SELAH'S
Stolen Dream

*One girl's victory is another's tragic defeat when two
girls can't divide the horse they both adore.*

Dedication

Thanks to the real Emma for the elements that brought the character Emma to life. This book is for you.

Thanks to my amazing SCBWI critique group, Charles Trevino, Mary Riser, and the cast of critters.

Thanks to my Face Book group, The Dream Horse Adventures Review Riders, for the encouragement to keep writing and for your support at book launch time.

Thank you to Butch Davis, retired from Texas and Southwestern Cattle Raisers Association, for the insight into horse theft.

Thanks to my husband, David, daughter, Sarah, and son, Christopher, for the constant encouragement.

I'm beyond grateful to my editor, Deirdre Lockhart, who has ridden any horse I've put her up on and done it brilliantly.

Glory to God. May the works of my hands bring honor to the house of the Lord.

Dear Reader:

If you enjoyed this book, please take a minute to help other people find it by sharing a simple review.

Sign up on my website for new release notification so you will find out about the next book as soon as it is available. Also, for any contests or giveaways— join me at http://www.susancount.com/

Hearing from readers encourages me to keep writing. E-mail a comment: susancountauthor@yahoo.com

Please like Susan Count at http://www.facebook.com/ susancount where I post only horse-related videos.

I'm also on Pinterest: https://www.pinterest.com/susancount/

SELAH'S
Stolen Dream

SUSAN COUNT

CHAPTER ONE

SELAH AND SWEET DREAM

*E*xcept for the dreary February weather, life was perfect. Absolutely, fantastically, completely—perfect. *Today, my dreams could come true.*

Today, Selah would show Sweet Dream in the biggest horse show in Texas.

And today might be the day she signed the movie contract for her and Dream to make a movie about their life. "You're going to be a star," she said to her reflection as she finger-combed her blonde hair and fixed a basic ponytail. "And Dream will be a famous horse star." She imagined people wanting her autograph. She'd have to guard the horse so no one snipped a wisp of her pink mane.

It all started when her instructor, Jordan, made that training DVD of her riding lessons on Sweet Dream. When they posted

1

it on social media, people quickly labeled it Cuteness Overload, and soon, it went viral. Then, after the wife of a movie producer watched Selah and Dream at an exposition, everything got supercharged. "Me—famous. Doesn't feel real. Pinch me."

On a day like today, she needed the perfect socks. It was a long-standing family conviction that mismatched socks were lucky. She hummed a happy tune as she tugged on one sock embellished with white unicorns and the other stamped with black horse heads. Balancing on the edge of the window seat, she admired her socks. "Sweet." She tapped her toes, flipped them outward and together again.

Out her second-story window, two horses slept in the dormant Texas Bermuda grass with their legs tucked near their bellies, and Sweet Dream's nose rested on the ground. The morning vapor shrouded the trees in wet mist while the sun gently lifted the night's shade. When a sure sign of spring, a robin, dropped to the ground near Dream, she jerked awake. The glossy black mare threw her head high and lunged to her feet. A snort accompanied her panic.

Dream's pasture mate, Buddy, rolled to his side and stretched out flat. The brown and white Paint was Grandpa's old show horse. Less than a year ago, Selah tracked down the gelding and brought him home. She'd hoped Grandpa would ride with her, but he'd gotten remarried instead. It worked out. Selah's family moved to the farm, and Grandpa and Grandma Katie lived on the farm next door.

Selah smiled at the rumble her two little brothers made scrambling down the stairs to breakfast. Living at the farm ballooned her heart with joy. She blew a kiss through the window to her equine pasture treasures.

The aroma of bacon drew her downstairs. The kitchen had gotten a fresh coat of paint, and, thank goodness, Mom had replaced Grandpa's ancient, three-tiered puffed curtains. Eight-year-old Davy and five-year-old Michael crowded together on one chair. Their heads tilted back, they dangled a piece of bacon and chomped like alligators. When Dad frowned at them, they turned into little gentlemen. Mom slid eggs from a frying pan with her back to the comedy.

Dad gathered his coat and his keys. "We'll drive in on Saturday and Sunday to see you show. Have fun, but stay close to Jordan. And please, take it easy on your grandpa." When the phone rang, he gestured to Selah. "Pick that up, would you?"

"Bye, Daddy. Love you." She waved at him. "Who would call so early?"

When she heard the movie producer's voice, her grin widened, and she wiggled her toes in her lucky socks. She held her hand over the mouthpiece and whispered to Mom. "Miss Cindy." She air-tapped at the phone like a woodpecker going after a beetle. Her mouth stretched wide in a silent scream.

Mom lifted Selah's chin to close her gaping mouth. "Boys, go find something to watch on TV," Mom whispered.

"For real?" Davy didn't wait for her to change her mind. Michael grabbed a piece of bacon for each hand before he raced after his brother.

Selah punched the button to put Miss Cindy on speaker so Mom could hear. "Contract! Today!" Selah's fists pumped the air. Without breath, she could hardly push out her words. "It's so exciting. We'll be movie stars."

"Are your parents available?"

"Yes, ma'am. Mom's here. She can hear you."

"Very good. When the contract arrives, your parents need to take it to a lawyer."

Selah fanned her hand, imagining a movie star about to faint. "So exciting."

"How did you get along with the script exploratory team?"

"We had tons of fun. They were crazy nice. They followed me and Sweet Dream around everywhere. Asked a million questions." She managed to breathe so she could continue. "Interviewed Grandpa too. He doesn't want to be in a movie but thought I was a natural. They thought Grandpa was a hoot and told me they got some great ideas."

"You completely charmed them. They said your grandpa was quite the character, but they were enormously leery of the horse." Cindy's contagious laugh had a charm of its own.

"Sweet Dream and I understand each other. The team wants the movie to open with a scene about how I found Dream tangled in wire with the buzzards after her. I don't see how that can work because Dream freaks at even the shadow of any bird—even a robin." Selah rattled on while wishing her voice didn't sound squeaky. She was a mature thirteen, but she sounded like a five-year-old shopping at the Breyer Model Horse Fest.

"They wouldn't do anything to scare or injure her. They have their ways of getting the scenes they need. A stunt horse, trained to do specific things, will handle many of the scenes, anyway."

She nodded along. "That makes sense."

"They are working hard on final edits and expect to be ready to roll soon. I'm setting up the screen tests for an actress to play you. Especially excited about two young actresses who are excellent riders. Once this last of winter blows through, I'll bring them to meet Dream before we finalize the selection."

"To play me?" Selah's spirit crumbled like burnt bacon bits. Her head itched right over her ear. "I thought—*I* would be *me*." Once she started scratching, other spots needed the same treatment. "Not just anybody can ride Dream." She sounded whiny now—worse than squeaky.

"We're buying your story, but I'll hire a professional actress for your character. Besides, didn't you tell me when you made the horse training DVD, your nerves were so bad the camera crew had to keep stopping?"

She sagged against the wall. "Well, yeah, but Mr. Cooper scared me before I got to know him. I don't throw up during filming anymore." *I know I can do it.*

"The pressure for a movie is intense. Besides, as darling as you are, you haven't had any professional acting classes. You'll be Sweet Dream's handler and advisor on her scenes."

"I won't be in the movie?" That familiar icky, acid, upset-stomach taste hit her mouth, proving Cindy's point. "I could take classes."

"Tell you what. I'll ask the team if they can write in a cameo for you. I'll be in touch soon. Bye now."

With her bottom lip protruding in a pout, Selah hung up. "I'm bummed. I wanted to be a movie star."

Mom tapped the tip of Selah's nose with her finger. "It'll still be an amazing experience for you."

Grandpa knocked on the kitchen door that used to be his own and pushed it open at the same time. "Is my movie star ready to go?" He smiled until he caught the look on Selah's face. "What happened?"

"They want Sweet Dream, but not me. I'm not a professional, and I throw up."

He dropped into a kitchen chair. "All that's true, sunshine. It's big business, you know."

She flopped into a wooden chair next to him. "I'm not giving up. I'll show them they need me. Dream and I are like that couple that dances in those old-fashioned musicals Grandma Katie loves.

We're perfect together. You wait and see. I'll be a movie star just like Sweet Dream."

"Fred and Ginger?" Grandpa scratched his head. "Thank you for watching those shows with her so I don't have to."

"It makes her happy."

"I love you to pieces, Selah, but you're delusional." Mom snuck a peek around the corner to check on the boys.

"I know. Shake it off and grow up." Selah could already taste the sweetness as she reached for a stack of oatmeal cookies. "Can we have cookies to take to the show? Oatmeal is Grandpa's favorite." She beamed at him.

As the plate slid by, Grandpa pilfered one.

Mom froze with the plate before him. Her eyes narrowed. "Only one?"

He waved away her concern and focused on Selah. "Trailer's hooked. Let's get the Selah show on the road."

"I'm ready. I just have to load Dream. Cooper and Jordan will arrive at the horse show by nine thirty, and they'd like me there about then." Selah stuffed her bag of cookies into a pocket in her suitcase.

"What's this? You've upgraded from a backpack?" Grandpa spun the pink suitcase and choked on a belly laugh when he spotted the watercolor portrait of Dream.

"It's a gift from Kingdom Saddlery. Don't you love it? I have to take a picture of Dream and me with it at the show. They want to use it in their advertising." Sponsored gifts had rained on her and Sweet Dream ever since Mr. Cooper released their training DVD. Suddenly, they were kinda famous in the horse world.

"Well, kiss your mom goodbye and put your fancy suitcase in the truck." Grandpa chuckled.

Selah's happy at setting off on new adventures with Dream paused momentarily—Grandpa left his cookie behind. He ate them any time of day, and he never missed the cookie tray in the church coffee zone. She snatched it for him, but something nagged at her. This wasn't right.

CHAPTER TWO

SELAH AND SWEET DREAM

*G*randpa stopped the truck at the gate to the horse show's equine parking area. A line of trailers, seven deep, stretched before them.

"Are you mad at me?" Selah fidgeted with the vent to turn the heat away.

"No." He searched her eyes. "Why in the world?"

"You haven't cracked one joke today."

A serious, thoughtful look deepened the wrinkles on his face. "Will you always remember me?" he asked in a hush.

She sat up and stiffened. "Of course."

"Knock knock."

Her fears faded when Grandpa cracked his joke. "Who's there?" Her muscles relaxed, and her hands unclenched.

"You forgot me—already?"

"Oh, Grandpa." She covered her silly smile with her hands and shook her head.

The security guard took the show registration forms, Grandpa's driver's license, and Dream's paperwork. The guard strolled to the horse trailer and compared the markings on the form to the horse. More trucks hauling horses lined up behind them. After what felt like forever, he handed everything back to Grandpa with a parking pass. "Have a great show." He triggered the gate to lift the entry barrier.

"Finally." She refolded the papers and stuffed them in the glove box. "They're serious about security."

"That gate check is about examining health certificates, not security. In my day, nobody had to worry. As Texans, we know from birth that horse theft is a hanging offense."

"Jordan said the colt Mr. Cooper's showing in novice reining is already worth over twenty thousand dollars. Mariah must be insured for a million dollars."

Grandpa eased the rig into a parking spot. "That's a lotta hay."

"We should get insurance on Dream. But she's worth so much more than money."

He reached across the truck and hugged her. "Sure she is."

"There's Jordan." Selah pointed through the maze of trailers at her riding instructor. Her gliding, ground-covering walk reflected her efficient nature. Even from a distance, Selah could tell Jordan had spent more time than usual fashioning a ponytail in her long brown hair. "I'll run and catch her. She'll know where Dream's stall is."

"I'll wait—"

Selah slammed the door on his last words as she raced after her trainer. Breathless, she hugged her. "I'm here. On time. Cute ponytail. Will you fix mine like that?"

"Turn around." Jordan tucked the end of Selah's ponytail under the rubber band and worked it upward through the gathered hair. "Very stylish, if I say so myself. And super easy. I've entered you in three more youth classes. Youth reining, showmanship, and barrels."

"Barrels! We've never run a barrel pattern." Selah gawked at Jordan like she was a complete stranger. "You're kidding, right?"

Jordan's eyes sparkled. "You'll be great at it and have fun too."

"What are you thinking? We can't do barrels. Those girls are smokin' fast, and Dream isn't interested in smokin'. People would laugh me right off social media. I'd never be able to show my face at school again."

"You'd be dead last. Ha!" They strolled past a row of stalls tagged with a denim-blue card blazoned with Cooper's Training Center.

Hands on her hips, Selah braced and pulled her shoulders back. "Not gonna happen."

"Lucky for you—I'm kidding." A smile spread across Jordan's slim face.

Selah slid open the door to a box stall with Sweet Dream's name written on the stall card. "You would've had to explain that to Dream. Running around barrels like she was shot out of a cannon is not her style."

"That mare is highly opinionated and prone to conserve her energy." Jordan scuffed her polished boot toe in the bedding. "I'll get more shavings in here." She pointed down the line of stalls. "Cooper's horses fill up the rest of this row. It'll be a busy week for all of us."

George, Selah's favorite van driver and wrangler, led a horse in from the trailer parking.

"Gringo's here. What a nice surprise." Selah rushed forward to take the gelding's lead rope. The buckskin horse that taught

11

her so much at Mr. Cooper's training center dutifully endured the hugging and sniffed her pockets.

"He gets all the hugs?" George kept hold of the rope and playfully tugged it back from her. "Don't start spoiling this horse already, little Miss Selah. Whenever he spends time with you, he acts like he doesn't have to listen to me." A smile crinkled his eyes as he handed over the lead rope.

"'Course I have a hug for you." Turning on the charm, she hugged him. "I've missed you."

"I've missed you too. When you're done spoiling him, put him in the stall. I've got to bring in the others." He wiped his hands on his new training center logo shirt.

"I told you, I'm not going to spoil him—oh! Too late." She lifted her shoulders and posed a smile, hoping to convince him she was innocent. "How did they get you to wear a T-shirt?" Even minus his green plaid shirt, his size made her think of the legendary lumberjack, Paul Bunyan.

"I don't want to talk about it," he grumbled and shuffled away.

Selah wiggled the lead rope to discourage the horse from searching Jordan's pockets. "Why is Gringo here?"

"Cooper wants you to ride him in a class that highlights the talents of mustangs."

"We get to show off. That's our superpower, isn't it, Gringo?" She kissed his muzzle.

"A group out of Nevada hopes to raise money to rescue as many as they can."

"Oh good. I guess it's efficient, but it's awful that the Bureau of Land Management rounds them up with helicopters." She hurried to put Gringo into his stall. "Grandpa's waiting—not too patiently by now. I should get Dream."

When she got back to Grandpa's truck, he lay back in the driver's seat with his always-clean hat slipped over his face—sound asleep. Tucked into the browband was a small blue feather Selah had found and declared a treasure when she was about seven. *Its sweet Grandpa kept my feather all these years.*

She untied Dream and backed her from the trailer. Her hooves clomped, making a loud racket and causing the trailer to vibrate. When she peeked into the truck cab at Grandpa, he was miraculously still asleep. "Poor Grandpa. I'll leave him a note and let him sleep." She tore a piece of paper off a show flyer in the tack compartment and tucked the note under the windshield wiper. "Come on, Dream."

All the way into the show barn, she talked to Dream. "We're so ready for this show. I'm nervous, but we'll make Jordan and Mr. Cooper proud. I didn't tell you—Cindy is sending the contract for the movie. I only get to be your staff. I'm way bummed, but you'll be amazing on the big screen."

Two high school girls snickered as they passed. Selah tucked her chin, suddenly interested in the blacktop as she walked a bit faster. "We don't care what they think. Do we, Dream? When you're a movie star, they'll beg to take a selfie with you."

She tied the mare in the back of the stall, slashed open a bag of shavings, and spread the fluffy pine bedding around. Three stalls down, George was busy stacking hay. "Thanks for the shavings. Can I cut the hay open for Dream?"

"Can't she go ten minutes without eating?" George tossed another bale from the cart.

"I'll give all our horses a leaf so I don't start a riot." Starting with Dream, she rushed from one stall to another delivering sweet hay. She paused a moment at Gringo's stall as he thanked her with a nicker and snatched a big mouthful. There was something so satisfying about watching them eat hay.

Dream's ears pricked toward the barn entrance, alerting Selah. Grandpa was moving fast like he had urgent bad news. His face was flushed. "Grandpa? What's wrong?"

"Did you unload Dream?"

"She's right there." She raised her arm and flipped her hand, pointing to the mare.

"And you didn't think you should tell me where you were going?"

She sputtered a defense. "I left a note on the windshield."

"I didn't see a note." Grandpa sank onto a bag of shavings outside Gringo's stall. He pulled off his Sunday Stetson and wiped the sweat from his forehead with his shirt sleeve. "Just scared ten years off my life."

"I'm sorry. You were asleep, and I didn't want to wake you. She's right here with me. Where else would she be?" She held up both palms.

He batted his hat with his hand and brushed away invisible dirt. "You can't be too careful at a big event like this."

"If someone was going to take a horse, they'd take Mariah. Which is probably why George sleeps on a cot in front of her stall." She chuckled at the thought. "Since Dream stays next door to Mariah, no worries."

As Grandpa lifted himself up, he wobbled a bit. He fingered the blue jay feather in his hatband before slipping his best hat securely on his head. "Katie's got me jumping at shadows because she had a bad feeling something might happen to Sweet Dream."

"She did? You didn't tell me." Selah crowded him and held tight to the front of his ironed cotton shirt. "What did Grandma Katie say?"

14

"Didn't want to scare you. She said it's probably nothing."

"What is nothing?" Selah tugged harder on his shirt.

He unclenched her fingers. "She sensed an angry spirit around Dream."

As George swept out the tack area, he promised, "I'll keep an extra-close eye on her. Though she's one mare that can take care of herself."

Wrinkling her brow, Selah glanced at Dream as the mare daintily nibbled wisps of hay from the feeder. George was right. "If Dream sensed an angry spirit, she'd stomp on it like she does snakes. Can we stop talking about it?" She shuddered. "It's giving me the creeps."

CHAPTER THREE

EMMA

Ten-year-old Emma sat astride the couch arm and cantered in sync with a girl, even younger than her, in a video. The pink ribbons in the girl's brown braids flapped behind her. The gray pony's legs fired like an engine in overdrive. At the approach of each jump, the girl thumped her boots on the pony's side and swatted it with a crop.

Her hands clinging to pretend reins guiding her imaginary mount expertly through the Speed Jumping event. She leaned into the turns and squared her pony to the jump. Gauging the canter strides to take off, she squeezed with her knees and balanced over her mount's withers. With a long moment of suspension, her imagination soared over the jump. Clear! She calculated the angle to the next jump. As the video pair nailed the last combination, she patted the couch jubilantly, praising her pony.

Mom tapped her shoulder. "Come on. We'll be late for your lesson." She switched off the TV.

Her parents always asked her to use her words, but she thought her voice sounded strange. Emma signed whenever she could get away with it. "I get so into watching her ride that I forget everything else." Her own riding lessons were too quiet, too slow, and too safe. They never had the excitement and energy of the girl in the video. But then the girl with the flying braids wasn't deaf.

Completely deaf in one ear, she couldn't remember a time when she didn't need a hearing aid in the other ear. Her parents told her she didn't lose her hearing until the year she started kindergarten. She had it, and she lost it. And the specialists couldn't tell them why.

She slipped on her riding boots, grabbed her safety vest and helmet, and flew.

Mom held out her jacket. "Bundle up. I don't want you catching cold."

"Yesterday, it was 72." As she stepped outside, Emma shivered.

"Today, it's 49. That's Texas. We never know what to wear."

As the February winds swirled the trees, a feed store delivery truck sputtered and rumbled outside the arena making it impossible for her to hear. While the hearing aid worked okay in small rooms, she found it useless outside. Even a slight breeze put so much static in her ear she had to turn it off. Her parents were saving to get her a higher quality one. Even though it was a pain, she wished they'd help her save for a horse of her own instead. But one dime at a time, she'd do it. She wasn't complaining. Not really. Because she had Pony-Boy.

She hung around the pony farm down the road until Mrs. Holmes recognized her as a horse lover and knew Emma wasn't going away. Mrs. Holmes graciously offered to give her a riding lesson on the old pony her college-age daughter had outgrown.

A big chalkboard hung in the center of the arena, attached to two jump standards. As she circled the arena at a trot to warm up Pony-Boy, she watched for Mrs. Holmes to write instructions on the board. Things like "relax your calf muscles" and "sink deeper into the stirrups".

For safety, Mom positioned herself at one end of the arena. Though Brianna didn't know how to sign or anything about horses, Mom insisted Emma's sister take her position at the opposite end of the arena. They would signal if there were any urgent instructions. *Like really, Mom? What could happen on Pony-Boy?*

Any horseback riding scared Mom, but jumping even little crossrails terrified her. The only reason she got to ride was because Dad insisted she do things hearing kids did. To get Mom to agree, she had to wear an ugly, bulky safety vest as if she were competing in upper-level, Cross-Country eventing. The helmet was strapped on so tightly she could hardly swallow. She was mostly deaf, but not helpless.

As she tightened the outside rein, she pressed her heel into the pony's side. He responded with a slow, controlled canter departure. If she didn't keep her leg pressure to ask him for each stride of the canter, sweet Pony-boy would decide it was time to quit and fall out of gait.

When Mrs. Holmes wrote *crossrails* on the board, Emma shortened her reins and pressed her heels deep in the stirrups. As she rounded the turn at the end of the arena, she steered the pony to the jump. Six strides from the jump, he felt bumpy or off balance. Something wasn't right. Then he smoothed out and cantered over the rails. It was fun, but compared to the girl with flying braids, it was slow motion.

As she made soft rein contact with the pony's bit, she held his head in the perfect vertical position. At her gentle request, he halted obediently. She'd hoped to ride him in horse shows someday, but it couldn't happen. His heart was willing, but twenty-eight was too old for him to take another child on the show circuit. Certainly not a speed event. She wrapped her arms around the Welsh gelding's neck, then blew a piece of his silky mane out of her mouth. "Thank you. You're the best." She kept her hug tight. "I so love you." After she slid from the saddle, she brushed his fluffy white hair from her safety vest.

Mrs. Holmes's lips moved. Emma wanted to get better at reading lips, but it was hard. The serious look on Mrs. Holmes's face told her it was an important conversation. As Emma went to learn the verdict, she walked in step with the pony. She knew in her heart what the farm owner was telling her mom and older sister. The precious, patient Pony-Boy needed to retire. She'd noticed the occasional hitch in his gait. It was time. He deserved acres of sweet grass and long naps under the sweet-gum trees.

She pressed on her hearing aid and focused on Mrs. Holmes's face.

"I'm sorry, Emma. I know we've been expecting this, but it's still hard. I wish I had another pony to offer you, but none of my broodmares are suitable."

Emma sighed and led Pony-Boy to the barn. She had to figure something out or forget about riding.

After dinner that night, she clutched her pony savings bank and made her way to Dad's office. Mom intently channeled her quilt piece along the guidelines on her machine and didn't look up as Emma passed. Dad smiled at her, closed his book, and set it beside him. "What have you got there?" he signed to her. As he patted his knee, she climbed into his lap. She hoped she would never be too big to be welcome on his lap.

She squeezed the rubber gasket from the bottom of the bank. "You heard I can't ride Pony-Boy anymore." When everything worked with her hearing aid, she felt the tones of her own voice. That gave her confidence she wasn't garbling the words. "He has arthritis." She puckered her mouth and made a super sad face. "I'm sad. I'll miss riding him." She extracted a wad of bills, unrolled them, and fanned them across the side table like a deck of cards.

"That's a lot of cash." He gestured. "That your birthday and Christmas money?"

She nodded. "And the chores I do for Mrs. Rose. I've saved three hundred, seventy-seven dollars and thirteen cents."

Dad exaggerated his facial features. "Whoa. That's impressive."

Emma giggled. She loved his silly faces. "Grandma sent me extra this year. She said she wanted a horse when she was ten too."

When his funny face turned into a frown, she worried. Without Dad on her side, there was no hope of convincing Mom. "Riding means so much to me." Her hands clasped together. Then she signed the words *so much*. "I feel like a normal kid." That was his soft spot, and her expression was a plea for understanding. "Even when I just think about riding, I smile because I'm so happy inside." As if to help him understand, she displayed the smile that riding put on her face.

His frown remained.

"We have a great pasture, and we don't really need a barn. Just a place to put tack and stuff. I'll do all the chores to take care of it." She watched his face for clues he might come around to her side, but only saw deepening wrinkles on his forehead. "I've almost saved enough."

Dad spoke directly to her good ear. "You know how your mom feels about you being near horses. She comes home from your lesson with her nerves frazzled. She worries that, if you fell and hit your head, you might lose what little hearing you have left. Have you talked to her?"

She sighed and twiddled her fingers in her lap. "Mom thinks I should learn to quilt and read books about other kids' exciting lives. I can ride as good as a hearing kid. I understand horses even better than hearing kids do. Horses talk with their eyes—the movements of their mouths and their ears. The way they hold their tails and how high they carry their heads. I've learned to listen to their body language."

"You are pretty clever." Dad pointed to the butter tub in her lap. "What's this?"

"My slime." She popped the top off and put the slime in his hand. "Everybody loves how soft it is. It's not expensive to make 'cause it's just cornstarch, glue, and water. I think I can sell a handful for three dollars and fifty cents. If I sell three, I'm ten dollars closer to owning a horse."

"This is my fault for giving you *The Black Stallion* series, isn't it?" Dad shook his head. "Figures."

"I was born with horse in my heart." She tapped her fist in the middle of her chest.

"I can see how important it is to you, and I can tell you've learned a lot. Would you like me to talk to Mom?"

"Oh, would you, Daddy? Thank you."

"I'll talk to her, but don't get your hopes up. Your mom and I need to be in complete agreement. Since protecting you is her superpower, I doubt she can be convinced."

That night Emma lay in bed planning and plotting how to convince Mom she should get a horse. When she felt rather than heard a thump, she sat up and reached for her hearing aid. She couldn't make out the words, but the fact she heard them told her parents were arguing. She scooted in the bed so her back tucked against the headboard. Then she drew her knees to her chest, clutched the bedcovers under her chin, and strained to hear. Why was everything always hard? After a few minutes, she tiptoed down the hall. The light was off in her parent's room. Dad must have given up on the idea of a horse.

CHAPTER FOUR

SELAH AND SWEET DREAM

*E*arly the next day, black barn swallows with white chests flitted in the rafters. The exhibitors bustled around eager for the show to start. Selah loved helping with the barn chores, and it was her turn to refill the horses' water buckets. To keep her nerves calmed, she focused on her tasks. As the flowing water gurgled, she held her necklace diffuser to her nose and breathed peppermint.

Jordan parceled out the vitamin supplements while George hayed the horses. After a rough night, Grandpa looked ragged. He said he didn't like motels. But he toasted the group with his coffee as he walked, deep in conversation with another old trainer friend.

Selah stepped into Dream's stall. "Good morning, beautiful. Hope you slept well. It's showtime."

Jordan breezed into Mariah's stall. "Selah, if you'd groom Gringo that would be a big help. I'd like you to ride him first today. I'm counting on him to be calm and show my colt there's nothing to worry about as I introduce him to the show craziness."

"Sure. I'll still have plenty of time to warm up Dream before her first class." After grabbing the grooming bucket, Selah went over every inch of the buckskin gelding. While he enjoyed his hay rations, she enjoyed the swelling excitement and activity of the show. She sniffed the air like a bunny. Somewhere close by, the sweet fried scent of a funnel cake drew her in. Her mouth watered as she pictured its powdered sugar dusting.

"I can't believe I'm here—with the best riders in the state," she confided in Gringo. "I hope I don't blow it."

Several girls down the aisle chattered playfully as they cared for their horses. On the other end of the aisle, a groom rattled and stacked feed buckets. After Selah saddled Gringo, she hung his bridle on the saddle horn. Jordan slipped on a grooming smock over her clothes and got to work on Mariah.

"Gringo's tacked up. Do you need any help with Mariah?"

"I was putting her bridle back together after I cleaned it and forgot it in the truck. I'd send George, but he needs to help the girls get the merchandise set up in the booth." Jordan unfolded a paper and checked an item off her list. "Would you mind? It's on the floor mat in the back seat." She tossed her keys as Selah slid Gringo's stall door shut. Selah caught the keys, spun, and strode out the exhibitor's door to the parking area. The sun glinted off the rows of trailers looking like her kind of jewels.

Her delight overflowed into sweet praise. Her spirit full of so much glee, she didn't want to contain it. Throwing her head back and her arms wide she twirled in joyful abandon. "Wow! What a wonderful day."

She dragged her fingers across the fender of her new trailer. The gift from Murphy Trailers came with pink lettering gracing the side. *Wonder if Sweet Dream's name will need lights around it when she is a movie star?* Her face lifted to the morning sun, and she skipped through the quiet parking lot. *Sweet joy.*

Three rigs over, Cooper's giant horse van took up four car spaces. She clicked the cab open. She easily found the bridle and slid it over the top of her shoulder. The bit hung at her waist.

Locking the truck, she retraced her steps. As she passed the rear of the rig, the hairs on the back of her neck tingled, but she saw nothing alarming. *Grandma Katie says listen to your instincts.* Still anxious, she lengthened her stride, and the bit slapped her hip bone with every step. *Calm down. I'm making a big deal out of nothing.* She slowed her pace. *I'm not gonna look like a scared rabbit and have people make fun of me.*

In spite of her resolve to be brave, her impulse to run won out. As she glanced behind her, she smacked into a cowboy.

He steadied, then released her. "Is everything okay?" The man didn't step back. But he smiled, and his face tightened as if he were concerned.

Even though with his jeans and rodeo buckle he looked like a harmless exhibitor, Selah sucked a step backward. "No. Yes. But I have to hurry and get this bridle to my trainer." She considered darting around a nearby horse trailer to get away from him.

He stepped aside. "I'm headed to the barns. I'll walk along with you."

"No thanks. Anyway, if I don't hurry, Grandpa will be out here looking for me." She again considered bolting, but he distracted her with a question.

"You showing or part of a support team?" His dusted brown leather boots fell in step beside her.

"Both." Her mouth dry and her neck stiff, she sidestepped discretely to widen the distance.

When they entered the barn, Jordan stowed the grooming bucket and reached for the bridle and the keys. "Thank you."

As Grandpa walked up to Dream's stall, the man turned aside as if to leave. "It's been a long time." Grandpa extended a hand to the man beside Selah.

"Ed." The man shook Grandpa's hand. "Yes, it's been longer than I can remember. I've not seen you since Mary passed. You stopped showing?"

Selah stood close behind Grandpa, but where she could see the man. *I guess he's okay.*

"Showing didn't seem important anymore. Remarried now. Thanks for coming to the funeral. It was nice of you." Grandpa put his arm around her shoulders. "This is Selah—my granddaughter. Selah, this is Cade Taylor."

"Nice to meet you," she obediently responded as Mr. Taylor nodded.

"Ah, I do see her grandma Mary in her."

"Everyone says that. She's also got Mary's ways with horses."

Mr. Taylor stood square with his thumbs tucked into the pockets of his starched jeans. He scrutinized the nearby stalls.

Grandpa swirled his coffee around the cup. "Mr. Taylor's been showing reining horses since—forever."

"You showing this horse for Cooper today?" Mr. Taylor asked her.

"Her Showmanship class is at two thirty, but she has classes tonight and all week." Selah squirmed, and Grandpa released her.

"I'll try to come watch today. She sure looks like Mariah."

Selah shrugged. "They're both black, but they don't move the same." She scooped up a wisp of hay and offered it to Dream.

"Say, I have a treat in my pocket. Can she have it?" He extended the horse cookie before she could even answer. Dream sucked it into her mouth and bobbed her head as she crunched it. Then she cocked her head and rolled her upper lip.

Bristling at his rudeness, Selah stepped between him and Dream. "We don't hand treat her." She assured herself it didn't matter and attempted to give a more mature response. She'd worked hard at putting being a self-centered brat behind her, but sometimes she still saw that side of herself that she wasn't too proud of.

"We use it in clicker training, but that's all. She gets pushy and will pull the pockets off your pants if she gets a chance," she explained with a light laugh. "I have a couple pairs of open-air jeans to prove it."

"Sweet Dream sounds like a character."

"How did you know her name?" The tightness in her neck returned. Was this man the evil Grandma Katie had sent the warning message about?

"It's on the stall door."

"Oh. Of course." Her face flushed.

Jordan called to her. "Mariah's ready. Grab your horse."

Selah jumped to sling open Gringo's stall door to bridle the gelding.

"Nice little horse, she's got there," said Mr. Taylor as she led the gelding out to stand with Mariah. With his eye on Mr. Cooper, he nodded at Grandpa. "Time for me to get. Say, where did ya find that coffee?"

Grandpa pointed to the back corner. "Follow your nose toward the cinnamon rolls. Selah's already checked out the food stalls. Tells me she has a hankering for a funnel cake."

29

Selah gave him her cutest scrunchy nose "oh Grandpa" look as Mr. Taylor strode off.

His face serious and intent, Mr. Cooper marched toward them. From his style to his manner, there was no mistaking he was in charge. His long legs devoured the distance between them. With a flip of his chin toward the rapidly departing cowboy, Mr. Cooper asked Grandpa, "What's he doing here?"

"I didn't ask. After all these years, isn't it time you two worked it out? He always seemed like a decent sort to me."

"Oh, we worked it out. I told him never to set foot on my ranch again. The man has problems I don't need around." He reached for Mariah's lead rope. "I'll take her into the warm-up arena. Bring along your colt." Mr. Cooper instructed Jordan and spun to Selah. "Good morning." He was off before she could even respond.

Still grumbling, Mr. Cooper led Mariah toward the arena. As Mariah disappeared through the crowd following Mr. Cooper, Dream trumpeted her dismay and moved anxiously around in the box stall.

Grandpa rubbed his balled fist in the middle of his abdomen. "I'm not feeling good. Think it's just indigestion, but I'm gonna go home. Another night in a motel will do me in."

She grasped his hand. "I'm sorry, Grandpa. Hope you feel better. I'm sad you have to leave."

He kissed the top of her head. "I know. Me too, but I'm worthless today. Your parents will be here later today to watch your first class ."

"They'll come back tomorrow too. Can you come in with them?"

He snorted. "Can you see me riding in the van between your two brothers?"

Laughing, she shook her head.

"Katie and I will drive down. We wouldn't miss your classes for anything. I'll be fine soon." He turned to Jordan. "I leave Selah in your very capable hands."

"She's always tailing me anyway." Jordan laughed, then expressed her concern. "You might think about going to a doctor."

Grandpa grinned, but said "no way" under his breath. He shuffled down the aisle, walking like a tired old man into the parking lot.

"Be okay, Grandpa. I love you," Selah whispered after him. The urge to chase him for one more hug was strong, but she shrugged it off. *Don't be a baby.*

She adjusted Gringo's tack and followed Jordan and her colt down the alley toward the riding arena. The boot rag Jordan had tucked in her back pocket swung with her quickstep tempo. "The colt looks great, but you have hay in your hair," Selah teased. Behind them, Dream whinnied and kicked the stall wall. "You're fine, silly girl. Eat your hay and hush. Mariah will be back soon."

CHAPTER FIVE

SELAH AND SWEET DREAM

At the warm-up-arena, Selah waited behind the crowd that gathered to watch Mr. Cooper work with Mariah. Before he swung into the saddle, he put the horse through all his signature exercises.

"Mariah can read his mind. She'll do anything for him, and she does it with pizzazz." Selah studied every move they made. "Dream and I will be that good someday."

Jordan snorted. "Shooting for the stars, are ya?"

"Just like you."

Mr. Cooper halted Mariah at the rail. "You don't need to wait on me. I'll take Mariah to the booth for her fan photo session. George will bring her back to the stall before you're done here."

Jordan nudged Selah. "Come on. Let's get to work," she playfully ordered as she fussed with the rigging on her colt's saddle.

Selah cued Gringo to circle around her on a long line. The mustang only needed a small reminder of his relationship with her. "He's all good." She settled into the saddle.

A few minutes later, Mr. Cooper waved at Jordan as he left and called, "I'm going to the booth."

As Selah eased Gringo around the arena, she let him look at each little dark corner and every flapping flag making sure he was comfortable. While the sturdy mustang jogged his pattern, she relaxed deep into the saddle and followed his cadence with her body. Riding Gringo was like putting on a favorite pair of shoes that had been lost in the back of a closet.

Jordan led her young horse into the arena and asked him to step backward smartly. Satisfied with his responsiveness, she tightened one rein to draw his head toward her and mounted the colt. Jordan drew in and released a deep breath and waited for the stud colt to do the same. When his ears turned to focus on her, she cued him to walk. "Gringo looks settled. I'm hoping he can teach little Camelot here all this is nothing to be concerned about." Jordan leaned over and snugged the girth one more time.

Selah positioned Gringo near to Camelot and slightly in front as if she were going to pony him like an outrider taking a racehorse to the starting gate. "The ring attendant told me they're going to open the main arena for schooling in twenty minutes."

"Oh, perfect. I was hoping to get him in there to look around before his first class."

"Camelot told me he won't embarrass you."

"Oh, he did, did he? Just so he doesn't panic and drop me." Jordan patted the young horse.

The practice arena filled with exhibitors working and exercising horses. A high-headed bay horse at the far end of the arena sped up, snorted, and snapped out a buck. Two other horses nearby threw their heads to the side and leapt away. Jordan's colt tensed, flipping his nose high. As he pranced a few steps, Jordan soothed him with her voice while pulling his head around to her boot until he stopped moving. Gringo's energy elevated, but Selah brought his attention back to her with only a slight touch on one rein.

As Jordan let the colt straighten out again, the out-of-control bay gelding gathered speed and raced along the rail. Before they could get out of his way, he charged between Jordan and Selah, knocking into Camelot. The young stud colt squealed as he reared and slammed Jordan's knee into the arena rail.

As pain washed over Jordan's face, Selah jumped Gringo forward to grab Camelot's bridle and snug him down. The colt trembled and crushed into Gringo.

When everything in the arena stopped, Jordan eased her foot from the stirrup and slid to the ground with a painful sigh. "Thank you for thinking so fast. That wreck could have gotten worse in a hurry."

Selah dismounted. "I know. What is wrong with that girl?"

"Stuff happens with horses." Jordan ran her hands over the young horse's body and legs. "Think he's okay. Just shaken up. I hope it hasn't wrecked his confidence."

"How can you not be furious?"

"I'm hurting and rattled, but I'm not angry." Jordan's fingers massaged her leg while she leaned to stretch. "It will add to my challenges for the week, but it was an accident. The rider is about your age and has only a fraction of your skills."

"That was awful for Camelot's first time in an arena."

"I need to get him back into the show arena as soon as possible to work through it. Otherwise, he's going to fall apart in his class. But first, I need to cut this session short and ice my knee."

"Stinks." Selah wrinkled her nose at the rider who caused the accident. "Let me lead Camelot. I can handle both horses, and you can be careful with your knee."

Jordan handed over the reins. "Thank you. That's very thoughtful."

With slumped shoulders, the girl who caused the accident trailed her horse as the trainer led him away.

"I bet they're going back into the round pen," Selah gloated.

"Never compare the middle of your journey to someone else's beginning. That was my grandmother's wise old saying. She was a huge football fan, and that quote came from some quarterback." Jordan snapped her fingers. "Tim Hiller! That was his name."

"Why are we talking about football?"

"Because like horses, football is a life of hard knocks. Why don't you go to the booth later and get a copy of the DVD we made of your first training sessions. If we're at the same motel, you two could watch it together. It would remind you of where you started."

"Ouch." Selah dropped her chin to her chest. She had been unkind, and that's not who she wanted to be. "You're right."

Turning onto their row, they passed through a group of riders hanging out on hay bales and folding camp chairs. Mariah's alarmed whinny followed by a double-barrel kick to the wall drew their attention.

"What's with Mariah?" Selah kept one eye on the mare as she tied up the stud colt. "Fuss. Fuss. That horse has such definite ideas on how she should be treated. If I didn't love her..."

Gringo's lead rope slipped from her hand. Her mouth gaped open and closed again. She jerked her head in short choppy movements, and her anxious eyes searched the stalls.

"Where's Dream?" Her chest tightening, she felt the blood drain from her face. She hurried down the aisle looking into all the stalls. As she spun back to Jordan, she attempted to crush her panic with a deep breath. "There's got to be a good reason she's not here. Does George have her?"

"He might have taken her outside to let her blow off steam."

Leaving Gringo standing in the aisle, Selah flew into Dream's stall and spun to search every corner as if nine hundred pounds of equine could hide. She struggled to suck in each strangled breath.

Jordan tossed both hands in the air. "I don't like the feel of this." She popped Gringo into his stall without unsaddling him.

Mariah threw her head down and bucked in place.

"Mariah is telling us something is horrible." Selah backed away in quick erratic steps. *Grandma Katie? Evil presence?* "She's got to be somewhere. George has her at the booth." When she spun to run to the booth, she fell headlong over a camp chair. Scrambling to her feet, she yelled, "Dream! Where are you?"

A groom in the next row paused in the door of his tack stall. As her fear escalated, he scanned the horses in his care.

When she bolted to find Sweet Dream, her frenzy spooked a horse being led in. It knocked its handler sideways and scattered a stack of buckets.

"Watch it," the girl yelled at Selah. Seeing Jordan, she yelled at her too. "You guys trying to get me killed?"

Selah pushed past the girl. "Sorry." Her heart ran before her to the booth. Dream had to be there. She must be getting her picture taken with her adoring fans. Spotting Mr. Cooper at the table, she sprinted toward him. She grabbed his arm holding a felt-tip pen, smearing his signature across a book page.

"What in the world, Selah? What is wrong with you?"

"Dream! I can't find Dream." She shivered uncontrollably. "Where's George?"

"Went to the van to get a box of books. He'll be right back."

"He doesn't have Dream?" Her throat tight, she barely choked out the words.

"No." Mr. Cooper shook his head, and his face contorted slightly, expressing his confusion.

Alarm rose like bile in her throat. "No!" She spun and pushed through the crowd, struggling to get back to the barn area. Her feet were so heavy she felt like she was running in muck. *This is all a horrible mistake. Dream can't be gone.* Back at the stalls, Selah threw herself around Jordan.

"She's not there either." Tears gushed. "They don't have her."

Jordan enveloped Selah in her arms and clung to her. "We'll find Dream."

George and Mr. Cooper rushed toward them. George scrutinized the area. "She wasn't here when I brought Mariah back from her photo session. I thought she was with you."

As her vision blurred, Selah gripped the bars on the nearest stall. She sank onto a hay bale. The flakes of hay separated, letting her slide to the floor. She leaned against the empty stall and closed her tear-filled eyes. When she opened them again, Dream would sniff her ear as if to ask why she was playing in her hay. But the empty stall door still stood open.

Please let this be a nightmare so I can wake up. A gasping sob escaped from her throat.

CHAPTER SIX

SELAH AND SWEET DREAM

Selah squinted hard to clear the pounding pain building behind her eyes as Jordan reached for her hand and pulled her to her feet. "Snap out of it. Now."

Mr. Cooper led the charge. "Everybody spread out and look for her," he ordered. "George and Jordan, get out there and search the parking lots." He pointed to the exit. "Selah, search the barns. Maybe she got out and somebody slipped her into a stall not knowing what else to do with her. I'll check the arenas and ask at the show office. Meet here in thirty minutes."

Mr. Cooper was right. She'd gotten loose. It was the only logical explanation. Selah struggled to stay focused. She hurried from person to person asking the same question. "Have you seen a black mare? Her mane has pink highlights." With each no, her exasperation grew, and she dashed to peer into the next stall.

Whinny, so I can find you. I'll know your voice. I'll come for you.

As everyone gathered at the stalls, she searched their faces. Jordan was tense and angry. George looked confused. "Any luck?" Her gaze lingered on them as she searched for hope.

They shook their heads. George dropped his chin to stare at the toes of his scuffed boots. Sweat from running through the parking lot stained his shirt. "No sign of her." He grabbed water bottles and handed one to Jordan.

"Is anything else missing?" Mr. Cooper scanned the area. He fixated on Jordan. "What's wrong with you?"

"A rider lost control of her horse, and he crashed into Camelot slamming me into the rail. I feel pretty lucky. All I got out of it is a super sore knee and a stiff back."

Anger hardened his tanned face. "George, check Camelot for injuries. Jordan, should we get you looked at?"

"I'm okay. I strapped on an ice pack with vet wrap. Makes walking an interesting challenge, but my knee isn't the biggest concern right now." Jordan adjusted the ice pack and turned to George. "Camelot and Gringo still have their saddles on. If you could take care of them, I'd appreciate it. I don't think I can lift a saddle right now."

George nodded and got to work.

"I should inventory the tack? We need to know if anything else is missing." Jordan limped away.

Mr. Cooper stuffed his hands in his jeans pockets and frowned with concentration. "Think hard." He examined Selah's face as if trying to see into her memory. "Do you remember latching the stall?"

"I–I can't remember," she stammered. "Her halter. Was on the hook—I think."

"I'm calling the police." He cut her off and dialed his phone. He strode with purpose, and people moved out of his way as he brushed passed.

She struggled to find the answer as he disappeared into the crowd. The whirl of show activities vanished from awareness, and she stood alone in her thoughts.

From the next aisle came a wail so high pitched it rattled the rafters. Selah felt all the girl's pain when she heard the scream of panic. "Batman!"

She got to the younger girl first and took her hand. "Your horse?"

The girl gulped air, but her voice squeaked out her horse's name. "Batman?"

"Mine's gone too. My trainer's calling the police. They'll find your horse. Don't worry."

Even favoring her knee, Jordan hurried to the girl. "Who's here with you?" She held the child as she cried and shook with fear.

"My trainer—main arena. I came—get—he's gone." The girl in braids choked out her words between sobs. She wiped the tears rolling down her cheeks onto the sleeve of her tailored show coat. "My pony was right here!"

Selah gripped the stall door to hold herself steady. She shuddered as she stared at the other girl experiencing the same nightmare. Her legs wobbled, and her hands trembled. With each breath, it got more real.

Slipping her arm around the young girl, Jordan guided her into the main barn to find her trainer.

Dizzy and nauseated—all in the same moment—Selah forced herself to take a deep breath. Even air couldn't stop the heaves racking her body as every bite of breakfast splattered across the concrete walkway. She tossed a couple handfuls of shavings to absorb the mess while Mr. Cooper returned empty-handed.

He waved George over. "Anything?"

She watched him expectantly, but already knew the answer was no.

"The show has their security guards searching the grounds." Mr. Cooper stuffed his hands in his pockets. "The police are on their way." He extended his phone, and she took it without a word.

"Grandpa. Something terrible has happened. Dream is gone. Can you come?" She sniffed. "I...need you, Grandpa."

When a police car appeared at the barn entrance, Mr. Cooper strode out to meet the police. Selah rose to her feet, her arms crossed over her chest and her teeth clamped down onto her upper lip.

The young officer shifted his heavy belt with both hands, adjusting the position of his weapon as he walked beside Mr. Cooper. His shirt stretched over his protective vest like he had Hulk muscles. His name tag read Officer Dalton. He rocked on the balls of his feet, studying the activity. Finally, he opened a small spiral and extracted a pen. "You reported a missing horse? Who is the owner?"

She stepped closer. "She's mine."

"When was the last time you saw it?" he asked the group.

"She was in the stall when I left to school in the arena."

Officer Dalton frowned as he hovered his pen over his notebook. "School?"

"It's horse training," Jordan explained politely.

"Do you have a picture?"

"Not here. I've taken a million on Grandpa's phone. He could send you one."

"In the meantime, can I get a description of the horse?" He scribbled a note in his book.

Selah patiently described the mare. "She's black with one white rear fetlock and a star on her forehead under her forelock." Her voice strengthened. "And pink-colored highlights in her mane."

"Pink." He moved only his eyes, flicking them to her and back to Jordan. "What's a fetlock and a forelock?"

Stepping to Gringo's stall, Jordan slid open the door. She grabbed the hair that hung from the top of the horse's head and between his ears, waving it at the officer. "Forelock." She spit the word out like bile, revealing her frustration. Grimacing in pain, she bent at the waist and pointed to the joint above the hoof. "Fetlock."

Officer Dalton walked into the empty stall. He examined the door. "Could the horse open this and wander off?"

"She didn't wander off." Selah swatted at a horsefly. "If somehow she had gotten out, she'd be hanging out with the horses she knows and tearing up the bale of hay in front of her stall. Every now and then, she would whinny for Mariah, but she'd be right here gorging on hay." She clenched her fists, wanting to pull out her hair. "I know her. Besides the whole barn would have been in an uproar if a horse got loose."

"Selah's right—a loose horse wouldn't go unnoticed." Mr. Cooper pressed his fingers on his jaw as if he had a toothache. "My team searched the grounds right after we discovered her missing."

"Okay. Is there anything else missing?"

"Her halter," she blurted.

With a bit of snark in her voice, Jordan didn't wait for him to ask this time. "That's something you put on a horse's head to lead and control them."

Officer Dalton turned to Jordan. "I've been an investigator for six years. Usually, I'm looking for missing children or an elderly person. I recover stolen cars and work bank robberies. As far as I know, no one in the department has any firsthand experience with horses. I appreciate your patience as I try to do my job."

"I'm terribly sorry." Jordan shifted her ice pack. "We're devastated. Not to excuse my actions, but the missing horse is a treasure and means the world to Selah."

"I understand." Officer Dalton's tone seemed a deliberate attempt to soothe her. "Have there been any strangers hanging around? Anyone taking an unusual interest in the horse?"

Mr. Cooper slapped his thigh with his hat. "Cade Taylor."

Selah straightened, but her voice wavered. "He was asking a lot of questions about Sweet Dream, and I had a bad feeling about him. It must be him!"

The officer stepped into the way of several riders squeezing behind them. "Excuse me. The horses over there belong to you?"

A girl in a bright-pink pearl snap blouse spoke up. "Yes. We're with the Walker County rodeo team."

"Did any of you notice anyone hanging around these stalls?"

"No." The girl looked at her friends. "We didn't notice anything."

A taller girl said, "Well, there was this one guy walking through the barn looking at the horses. I noticed him because I turned around real fast and almost spilled my drink on him. He had on a white Stetson and a big belt buckle like a calf roper."

"Was he wearing a dark-blue shirt?" Jordan asked.

"I don't know, but his eyes were blue. And he was super nice." She giggled. "I didn't see where he went because Lindsey started teasing me about having a crush on an older man." She elbowed the girl next to her and giggled again. "Then we all went to the main arena."

"Sounds like Taylor. He thinks he's quite the ladies' man. He used to work for me," said Mr. Cooper. "He was here earlier, but left as soon as he spotted me coming."

"The man scared me in the parking lot and then followed me into the barn." Selah looked from one to the other in numb disbelief. "You have to find that man—he's got my horse."

"I'll file a report, and someone will contact you if we need more information." The officer slid his notebook in his pocket. "I'll do what I can."

She took a card with his name on it. "That's it?" The police would never find Dream. Her jaw clenched, and she bit a sore spot inside her cheek. She tasted blood.

Reaching out to shake his hand, Mr. Cooper thanked the officer before he left to interview the other people in the barn with missing horses.

Jordan sank into a chair in front of Dream's stall and adjusted her ice pack. "I've never felt so helpless in all my life."

Selah wanted to collapse next to Jordan. "How can this happen? We have to do something—fast—or I'll never see Dream again." Her teeth clamped together so hard her jaw hurt.

Mr. Cooper rested his hand on Selah's shoulder. "I have an old friend who is a livestock ranger with the Cattleman's Association. He's been investigating horse theft cases for twenty years. He's on his way."

Katie expected this. She tried to warn me. If only I'd taken her seriously. I should never have let Dream out of my sight.

CHAPTER SEVEN

SELAH

Selah sat curled in a ball in the corner of Dream's empty stall. Her arms propped on her knees, and her hands covered her eyes. George's cough disturbed the black silence in her brain as he shifted in the camp chair in front of Mariah's stall. Too late for Dream, but the other horses were under twenty-four-hour watch now. *My Sweet Dream's in a strange trailer with other strange horses. Has he hurt her? She must be so scared! Why did we ever come here?*

"Selah." George spoke tenderly to her. "You need to come out now. The ranger's here. Mr. Cooper is signing books in the booth, but he wanted to know when the ranger got here so I'm headed to get him."

She blew a deep breath out through her mouth and rose to her feet, brushing the shavings from her jeans. She walked with the same weakness she remembered from having the flu. Completely drained of strength, she shuffled to the stall door and collapsed into a camp chair.

Striding toward her was a short man wearing a black vest with an official patch over his heart. His dingy shirt looked like he'd picked it up off the floor to put it on. His face was round like Santa except it wasn't cheerful. The man glanced at his pocket-sized notebook and then to the numbers on the stalls before stopping in front of her.

She stood and jabbed her hands under her armpits. "Can you find my horse?" Her throat felt thick and her voice flat and emotionless. She stared, unseeing, at the stall latch across the aisle. "You have to find her."

"That's why I'm here. You must be Selah?"

She snapped to attention. "You have to find her. She's the only horse for me. I can't lose her."

"So, what do you know?"

"She was here, and somebody took her. Why would anybody take her?"

"When we figure out who, we'll know why."

"George went to get Mr. Cooper." She studied the ranger. He searched all his pockets and finally pulled out a little, sawed-off yellow pencil like you'd use for miniature golf. Despite his official agriculture department patch, he hardly seemed like an expert on missing horses. While they waited for Mr. Cooper, the man examined the area and made notes. His notebook might have survived being run over by his truck. The cover was partially torn from the spiral, and one corner bent like a tab.

Hurrying toward them, Mr. Cooper stuck his hand out to the ranger. "Thanks for coming, Butch."

The man reminded her of someone. But who? Then it hit her. That silly detective show Grandpa loved. The investigator wore a rumpled overcoat. The bad guy never took the detective seriously and always got tripped up in a lie. *If only life worked out like TV shows.*

"Mr. Cooper has a lead for you to track down." She tilted her chin up and spoke with authority. "There was a man here earlier that he fired. Cade Taylor. George saw him walking through the barn looking at horses."

"Selah's right. My money's on Taylor." Mr. Cooper untucked his thumb from his pocket and hooked it toward the neighboring stalls in the next aisle. "There was a horse stolen from over there too. According to the show office, there's a total of three horses missing."

The ranger held open a notebook. He wet the tip of his pencil. "Today's the twenty-ninth, right?" Without waiting for confirmation, he said, "I'm always glad when February is over. So, what else can you tell me about Cade Taylor?"

She stiffened. "He was sneaking around our horse trailers. He made me nervous. Then he talked to Grandpa."

Mr. Cooper gazed into the barn rafters where a cowbird heckled the barn swallows. "I wonder if he took Dream thinking she belonged to me."

"He said Dream looked like..." She lost her train of thought. "Like Mariah. Maybe he saw taking her as a chance to get back at Mr. Cooper for firing him."

"Why did you fire him?" the ranger asked.

"Smoking in the barn. Grown man should know better. Never could trust him afterward."

"Could be trying to get even with you, and then took the other horses to cover his trail. Or it could be it was just an ordinary horse thief, and she was the easiest target. Is she tattooed, chipped, or branded?"

Selah shook her head and scowled. "And that man fed Dream a treat so she'd trust him."

"At this point, miss, Cade Taylor is only a person of interest. Best to keep the investigation wide open rather than focus only on one person." Butch redirected her attention. "An obvious mark of ownership can deter a theft. Was she wearing a halter?"

"I never leave her with a halter on—it's too dangerous. I take the best—best care..." Her voice faltered.

"You're right. It is dangerous. A halter can hook it on things like stall latches, and they'll panic." Even as Butch responded to her, he never stopped scanning the area.

"Her halter was hanging right there on the hook." Selah flipped her hand toward the empty space where the halter should've been. "I've looked everywhere for it, and it's gone."

"Considering his past connection to Cooper, I'll investigate Taylor thoroughly. But it could have been anyone. Your horse might have been selected at random. Thieves usually look for a horse wearing a halter or with one hanging right outside the stall. The aisle must have been clear and quiet. Folks who operate like this look for an easy mark."

She groaned and pushed herself to remember anything that might help find Dream.

"Though they've been known to stride in with a halter and lead rope over their shoulder. Put it on and lead a horse away. So quick nobody takes any notice. Most natural thing in a big show barn are people dressed like they belong and leading horses around everywhere."

She slowly shook her head as she realized the truth he shared.

"Have you talked to the owners stabled near you? Did anyone see anything?"

"The police talked to them." Selah pointed to a group of girls. "They saw an older man. The only thing they said was he had blue eyes and a white cowboy hat." She closed her eyes and shuddered.

"They couldn't remember the color of his shirt. Mr. Taylor was wearing a blue shirt."

"I'll want to talk to them."

"The pony stolen from over there belonged to a little girl. It's a champion junior hunter. Poor thing went home with her trainer right after they talked to the police. The other stolen horse was a cutting horse stabled in the barn next to ours."

"That's important because that makes it less likely it was someone with a grudge against Mr. Cooper." Butch wrote notes in his little book. "So three horses. Means all he has is a three-horse trailer or he got spooked and got out with what he had. Did anyone see Mr. Taylor's trailer?"

Mr. Cooper asked, "Selah, you were in the parking lot with him. Do you know?"

Pressing her fingers into the bony ridges over her eyes, she thought hard. It was only a few hours ago, but it felt like forever. Finally, she shrugged. "I was near my trailer. I never saw where he came from." She hoped the investigator could read his notes later because they looked like scribbles to her.

"Jordan, when you talked to Mr. Taylor, did you find out why he was here?"

"No. But Ed, Selah's grandpa, spent the most time talking to him. Maybe he knows."

Mr. Cooper snapped his fingers. "George, would you go to the show office and ask if Cade Taylor is a registered exhibitor? The girl with access to that information wasn't there when I went. If she's still not there, tell the show manager I want her found."

"Yes, sir." George gave a quick nod and steamed toward the show office.

"Is there anything else missing?" Butch looked around.

"What matters is Dream is missing!" Selah's faint, squeaky voice bordered on hysterics. *You can't be for real.*

Jordan put her arm around Selah and spoke directly to Mr. Cooper. "At first I didn't see anything out of place in our tack room, but I'm afraid the bridle and matching breast-collar that you use in the grand entry parades are gone." To the ranger, she said, "They're hand-tooled with silver trim and conchos."

"Good. If we can find the tack, we might get lucky and pick up a lead." Butch tapped his pencil onto his tongue and wrote in his book. "Can I get a picture of the tack? And I'll need good pictures of the horse. Both sides. Front and rear."

Selah's whole body felt weak, and talking loud enough to be heard took too much effort. "My grandpa... is... bringing some."

Rubbing his forehead, the ranger wrote again in his notebook. He leaned his head, stretching his neck from one side to the other.

Had he ever actually found a stolen horse? He didn't look like he could find his own wallet. But she didn't dare ask. She needed to keep this man on her side. "What does he want with Dream?"

Butch rapped his pencil on his book. "Generally, a thief is looking for a quick profit. He would take the horses to an auction barn somewhere."

"Wouldn't he have to prove he owns her?"

Butch shook his head. "Sadly, no." He ever so slowly detailed his notes. "Do you have a bill of sale for your horse?"

"I don't think so." Her frown deepened.

"Most people don't. If the horse is in your possession, it's assumed to be yours."

She stared into the empty stall. "Dream is out of my grandmother's dressage mare."

"A professional thief can fake a bill of sale. Most places aren't going to ask for even that to put the horse into auction. Some will ask for proof of a clear Coggins test, but not all. The sale barn can run a Coggins or the thief can fake one. If you know what you're doing, it's not difficult. And with three horses gone, it's clear this guy knows what he's doing."

"Dream isn't your average horse. She isn't easy to handle." A thread of hope teased the corners of Selah's mouth into a smile. "No one will buy her."

"I'm sorry to tell you it happens all the time." Butch patted down his other pockets when the lead on his stubby pencil broke. "Thieves use drugs to make her look like a docile child's pony. Until the new owner gets the horse home."

No! She stomped her foot. "That Taylor man fed Dream a treat before I could stop him. I bet he gave her something to keep her quiet. He couldn't have dragged her away from me unless something was wrong with her."

"Normally, it's an injection."

"He had to give her something to even lead her away, which I have a tough time seeing, but he'd never ever get her into a trailer."

Butch didn't look up from his notes. "Sedation, blindfold, and a butt rope."

George rejoined the group, and everyone waited to hear what he'd learned. "Taylor's not an exhibitor."

"Why was he even here?" She couldn't keep the whine out of her voice. "Where is he?"

"I've no idea how to find him. I haven't seen him in years and really thought he'd left the state." Mr. Cooper folded his arms across his chest and walked away.

"My grandpa should be here anytime, and he'll know what to do. He won't stop until we find Dream."

CHAPTER EIGHT

SELAH

Selah turned as Grandma Katie marched into the barn with Grandpa lagging behind her. In spite of her small size and glowing yellow flowered blouse, there was no doubt she was here for answers. Selah ran to them, flew into Grandpa's arms, and wailed. "Someone took Dream." Tears streamed down her cheeks as she clung to him.

"I know, sunshine." He stroked her hair. "We won't rest until we find her."

Grandma Katie rubbed Selah's shoulder as she cried into Grandpa's chest. "Stealing a living, breathing creature that can't defend itself is heartless."

"You tried to warn me." Selah squeaked between sobs.

"This is not your fault," Grandma Katie's hand stilled. "And I didn't have any more to go on than sensing an evil presence."

Grandpa bent to look Selah in the eye. "I'm sorry I wasn't here."

She bit down on her bottom lip. "The investigator's waiting to talk to you."

Grandpa strolled along with his arm around her. She'd never known him to walk so slowly. When they finally got there, he shook hands with Butch and slipped into a camp chair. "Need to take a load off." His voice was a little shaky.

Katie hovered behind him for a minute, then got him a bottle of water from the ice chest in front of Dream's empty stall. Looking at him, Selah was beginning to worry she might have a bigger problem than even Dream being missing. "Grandpa? Are you all right?"

He took a small sip of water. "Don't you fret about me."

Mr. Cooper stuffed his hands in his pockets and bent toward Grandpa. "Sorry you had to come back, Ed. It seems you spent more time talking with Taylor than anyone. Butch has some questions for you."

"Katie and I wanted to be here for Selah."

"Do you know why he was here?" The ranger asked.

"Not exactly. We talked about two colts he's training. I figured he was showing 'em."

"Did he say anything that might give us a clue where to find him?"

Grandpa scratched his head and took a gulp of water. "I don't remember anything like that. He told me he was working as a long-distance horse transporter more than he was training."

"Did he mention the name of a company, or is he on his own?" Butch flipped the pages in his notebook and reread his notes.

Selah pressed on her eyes with the heels of her hands. Long-distance! He could be anywhere by now. *He can't just take my horse and disappear.*

Grandpa shrugged. "Actually, I did most of the talking. He'd met Selah in the parking lot. Once someone gets me talking about her, you can hardly get me to stop." He slid his hand around the base of his neck and grimaced as he worked the muscles. "I was telling him about Selah getting her dad a job in Canaan so she could move into *my* farmhouse." He tilted his head toward Gringo. "Taylor thought the buckskin was Selah's, and I didn't get to correct his impression. When Taylor saw Cooper coming down the aisle, he got real fidgety and scooted out of here fast."

"You're right." Selah slapped her hands onto the side of her head. "Jordan told me to get *my* horse and come with her. I knew she meant Gringo, so he's the one I got out of the stall. Mariah is so famous she'd be hard to sell. He thought they looked alike so maybe he took Dream thinking she was Mariah's offspring."

"I only follow your logic up to a point," Mr. Cooper said. "He also took two other horses that couldn't be mistaken for mine. Besides, I have six more horses on this aisle." He put one hand on the stall and the other on his hip while he tapped his toe. "Doesn't make sense."

The ranger dug in his pocket when his phone rang and clicked it off. "If he's nursing a grudge, maybe he took the horse he thought might hurt you the most. Left the others so it wouldn't be obvious it was a grudge. If he thought Dream was a daughter of Mariah and your next show prospect, that'd do it."

"It definitely would," Mr. Cooper agreed.

As the adults talked around her, Selah lost focus. *How could this happen?* She squeezed her eyes tight and shuddered. *No tears.* She needed to be strong for Dream.

"Why make a trip to the sale barn with only one horse in the trailer, even if it's the primary target. Fill 'er up." The ranger scanned the expansive barn. "They steal one from different areas of the barns so they're not seen by the same folks. If people only see 'em once, they're not likely to take much notice." Butch tucked his notebook into his shirt pocket. "The theft of the other two horses could be a cover-up for a revenge theft against you, or it might be completely arbitrary."

Her jaw tensed, and her outrage boiled over. "How could anybody be so mean?"

"They don't conform to the laws the rest of us live by." The ranger repositioned his hat. "Career con artists are superficially charming. They're masters of befriending you—gaining your trust. These predators lack remorse." He glanced at her, rolled his lips inward tightly, and popped them apart. "Sadly, even if it's stealing from a young girl."

She slid onto Grandpa's knee and collapsed against him. He wrapped both arms around her and held her like she might fall from his lap otherwise. His breathing seemed a bit raspy, and his cough shook her. She tried to listen to the investigator. She knew it was important, but her mind kept slipping away. *Dream, where are you? What has he done to you?*

"I need a best guess on what time she disappeared," the ranger said. "Jordan, can you help me with that?"

"Sure. We tacked up three horses, Mariah, Gringo—the buckskin over there—and Camelot—the colt I'm training. When we left for the practice arena, Dream was fussing about being separated. It was about eleven fifteen."

George said, "When I brought Mariah back, it would have been almost twelve fifteen. Dream was gone then, and I thought she was with Selah."

"Over an hour gives the thief plenty of time." The ranger tipped his head toward the empty stall in the next aisle. "I'm going to poke around here, establish the time frame for the disappearance of the other two horses, and see if your Cade Taylor is a common denominator."

Mr. Cooper groaned like a horse heaving itself off the ground. "You've got my contact numbers. Keep us informed."

"Will do. Soon as I finish here, I'll go to the office to start the reporting process. If the inspectors come across anything, I'll let you know. Sometimes, the sales barn manager suspects a horse is stolen, and they'll check to see if a report's been filed. They want to protect their reputation. I'll do what I can, but I don't have much in the way of resources."

"I don't understand." Selah alerted and sat up tall. "It sounds like you take her picture, stick it on a board, and wait to see if someone reports a found horse."

"We'll put her description on a list that goes to the sales barns and border checkpoints for the vans headed to the slaughterhouses."

She leaped to her feet. "Slaughterhouses! Somebody might kill Dream?"

"No. No. It's just procedure. She's a high-quality healthy horse. An unscrupulous seller will act like her life is in danger. Then people with good hearts will pay a lot to save a horse they think is destined for a kill pen. They never realize their purchase allows the thief to buy three or four other horses that don't have any value in the pet market."

"I truly don't understand." Grandma Katie had listened politely long enough. "Horses are beloved and romanticized by the media. Yet there is a whole underworld—and unspeakable cruelty."

"Nobody who loves horses understands this," Jordan agreed.

"I'm sure Selah's horse will show up at a sales barn sooner or later. If she doesn't sell at the first barn, she'll be trucked to another one. My team will be watching for her."

Jordan said, "You can't sell at auction and get near what the horse is worth."

"They'll try for a private sale first. Either way, for the thief—it's pure profit." Butch walked into Dream's vacant stall and scanned the area.

"I can offer a reward for the mare," Mr. Cooper suggested. "If that helps."

Grandma Katie immediately agreed. "Great idea. We'll put up money for the reward too. Whatever it takes to find my granddaughter's horse and put the thief in jail."

"The thieves don't tend to rat each other out. The contracts they get from the slaughter companies are lucrative, and they protect their racket." Butch scooted his toe in the shavings around the edges of the stall. "A reward is good for buzz though—getting people to share the post on social media."

Selah's world drifted out of control even for the grown-ups she'd always counted on. Her life's story was being written and directed around her, and she felt helpless to change it. Overwhelmed and numb, she closed her eyes in danger of losing all hope.

Grandma Katie put her hand up like a traffic cop. "I think we've heard more than enough on the horror. Can we focus on how to find Dream, please?"

"Yes, ma'am. You're quite right."

"Call me about any lead you get." Mr. Cooper braced his feet. "Let's make the reward big enough to get that horse back."

"Thank you." Hopelessness made her voice meek.

"Your call." Coming out of the stall, the ranger shook the bedding off his boots. "I don't see anything helpful here. I'm sorry to say the lack of clues gives it the earmark of being a pro's job."

"I've got to get back to the sales booth." Mr. Cooper's frustration put a growl in his tone. "You find Taylor, and you'll find Dream. Let us know what else we can do." He turned to Selah, opened his mouth to speak, but gave a quick shake of his head instead.

Grandma Katie took Selah's hand and led her to the exit. "Come on, sweetheart. There isn't anything else we can do here. Let's get you home."

"I can't leave without Dream." Pain gripped her heart.

Jordan's voice trembled as she slipped her arm around Selah. "I know it's impossible to believe, but she's not here."

Selah pulled away and faced the group. Her swollen eyes felt like slits. Her tears gouged forever scars on her heart. "I can't go! I won't leave her." She wiped her sniffles across the back of her hand, but didn't budge. "She needs me."

"There's nothing more we can do here." With her voice soft and gentle, Katie urged Selah toward the truck.

Grandpa shuffled along behind them.

"If you hear anything, call me right away."

"I promise." When Jordan hugged her, Selah clung to her. As Jordan helped Selah into the back seat, Katie opened the passenger side door for Grandpa. He leaned on her as he eased into the seat and she shut the door. Then he dropped his favorite hat into his lap and laid his head back.

As Katie started the engine, the oddness of it all crept into Selah's consciousness. "You're driving?"

Katie's glanced in the rearview mirror and caught Selah's eyes for a minute before she shifted into gear without answering.

Grandpa's just got a cold or something. He'll be better in no time. Grandma Katie healed his Paint horse, and she'll fix him up good as new. Then he can help me find Dream.

Selah couldn't help but glance back. The barns glowed with yellow light. Inside, the stalls were full of horses, and their people hustled about tending to them. The excitement of the horse show went on as if nothing had happened. *A few hours ago, my life was perfect too.*

CHAPTER NINE

SELAH

Selah stared into the darkness of the long country road. How did the day go from amazing and perfect to the worst day of her life?

Please come home to me. She sniffled.

When Katie parked in front of the farmhouse, the lights were on in the kitchen. Through the window, Selah saw her little brothers dipping graham crackers in milk. Her body felt limp and heavy. When her dad walked down the path to the truck, Grandpa rolled down the window.

"Anything?" Dad asked.

Grandpa shook his head.

"Get some rest, Dad. You look worn out. I could have gone to get Selah. We were already planning to drive down today."

"I wanted to go. I needed to talk to the livestock investigator." Grandpa shut his eyes and dropped his head against the seat rest.

Katie leaned over where she could see Dad. "I'm taking him home to pamper him right now."

Dad patted Grandpa on the arm and opened the truck's back door for Selah. When she didn't bounce out, he took her hand and led her to the house. Inside, the lights were too bright, and she squinted. Mom offered her soup, but she shook her head and looked away. The boys quieted. Selah lifted one foot and then the other to make her way up the stairs to her room.

She plopped onto the end of her bed and peered into the night through the window overlooking Dream's pasture. Flopping onto her side, she curled into a tight ball. When she covered her face with her hands, they smelled like horse, and she began to sob.

Sometime in the middle of the night, she woke. Someone had covered her with her softest pink blanket. Her eyes felt puffy and her nose stopped-up. She pulled the small chain on a unicorn desk lamp, and a tiny pink bulb cast a cozy glow of light over the room. A piece of paper more rumpled than folded lay on her desk. Davy had drawn a crude black horse and Michael a pink-crayoned heart. In spite of her pain, she smiled. She tacked them to a cushioned board and climbed back into bed. She tried to read a book, but couldn't concentrate and gave up. Was Dream awake somewhere?

The house was still. Then Selah remembered it was Serve Your Community Sunday at church. After worship service, her family would be making repairs and painting a retired librarian's house. Grateful to have quiet, she wandered from one room to another, one window to another. Turning on the TV, she searched for a news channel. Surely, there would be reports of the horses stolen from the show. But the heads on the screen droned on about political investigations and corruption. As the hours passed, her weary grew, and she slept again. The family bursting through the kitchen door scared her awake. "Dream!" She sagged against the cushions.

Mom sat beside her and put an arm around her shoulder. "Having a tough day?"

When all Selah did was nod, Mom added, "Why don't you get dressed and take a walk? It's brisk outside, and it will clear your head."

Selah dutifully went through the motions of life. In her more clearheaded moments, she worked on a plan for finding Dream. *I'll call the president if I have to.*

Even after her walk, she couldn't eat dinner and opted for a piece of cinnamon toast. She tried to read, then tried to watch TV, then tried to read again, but nothing soothed her. Even sleeping didn't quiet her mind.

When she startled awake for the third time, she knew she needed Pearl. Though Grandpa had started allowing the cat into the house, everything changed after he married Katie and moved next door. Selah's family moved onto Grandpa's farm, and having two boys flying around the house was too much for Pearl. She'd relocated her little self back outside to the barn.

The house was dark so Selah tiptoed down the stairs, avoiding each squeaky spot. She gently lay the screen door closed and went in search of her cream-colored purr.

Her heart jumped at the soft nicker greeting her. She sucked in a breath. "Dream?" But in an instant, she knew that voice, and it wasn't Dream's. Grandpa's old Paint horse, Buddy, thrust his big head over the stall door. As she wrapped her arms around his neck, she sighed. Her face buried in his rough mane, she closed her eyes and clung to the memory of hugging Dream's neck. "She's gone, Buddy. Somebody took her." Telling Buddy out loud sunk all hope that this was only a nightmare. When she realized how hard she was squeezing him, she loosened her grip but kept her face buried in his comfort as she sank into grief and despair.

The odds were Pearl was sleeping in Dream's wooden feed box. Dream often slept right by the cat. Unlatching the gate, Selah eased into the dark stall. For a moment, she imagined a movement in the attached paddock, but her blurry eyes were not seeing her mare.

"Pearl." Selah reached into the bin and scooped the sleeping feline from her dreams. "Are you waiting for her to come home too?" She hugged the cat and slid to the stall floor, pressing her back to the wall. She remembered trying to befriend Dream in this very spot. The wild, frightened horse had snatched the offered carrot, but slammed her into the wall. With Grandpa's help, she'd won the horse over. Or had the horse won her over? That was never really clear.

She peered into the darkness. The day Mr. Cooper's van arrived for Dream's trip to his training center, their whole world changed. After Mr. Cooper released the training film featuring the pair to his fans hungry to learn his techniques, he'd made them celebrities. And Jordan—Selah thought of her as a big sister. Her calm, kind ways supported Selah through some tough lessons, not all of them on a horse. *Jordan won't rest until Dream is home.* But her hurt knee was sure to slow her down, and she'd be crazy busy at the horse show all week. Dream would be gone forever by then.

What was wrong with Grandpa? Grandma Katie never drove. Why was he so tired? For now, Grandpa wouldn't be able to help, and Grandma Katie would be busy taking care of him. She was a wonderful nurse. Without her, Grandpa's old Paint horse wouldn't have survived. Selah was grateful, though Grandpa never did start riding again, even with all her begging. His new life with Katie kept him busy enough, he said. They were traveling a little, but had yet to go on Grandpa's dream trip to Israel. When Katie slipped brochures about Ireland next to his morning coffee, the itinerary expanded. Katie said her Irish ancestors raised sheep. *I shoulda figured.*

Selah needed to keep thinking about who could help find Dream. Her parents would be supportive in the search, but they didn't know anything about horses and wanted to keep it that way.

She ran her tongue over a split on her lip. Her mouth felt like a dried-up kitchen sponge. Even with the warmth of the cat, she shivered in the drafty stall.

She dragged Illusion's ratty old fly sheet down from the top rail. Miss Laura had sent it for Dream. She'd said it was to give Dream courage. Well, Selah needed it. She wrapped the sheet around her shoulders, barely disturbing Pearl, and waited for courage.

Miss Laura! She'd raised Sweet Dream out of Grandma Mary's dressage mare. Miss Laura would help her find Dream. She never gave up when Dream was lost in The Canaan Grasslands. She wouldn't give up now.

She wished the video would rewind so when the sun came up she would see Dream grazing in the far pasture. When she called the mare's name, she'd throw her head high and stand with her neck stretched and her ears pointed toward Selah's voice. How many times had it happened in just that way? In a blink, she would explode into a canter, tossing her head and leaping like a frisky fawn. If it was cold outside, the mare would throw in a buck of wild joy. She pictured Dream slowing to a trot and lowering her head, her muzzle extending in a polite question. "Carrot?" Selah would offer her the highly anticipated treat and rub under the mare's thick mane.

Hours later, still wrapped in the fly sheet, she slipped into the farmhouse, cradling Pearl, and dialed Miss Laura. When the answering machine picked up the call, Selah left an urgent message and hung up. She immediately dialed again. "I forgot to tell you we think the man who stole her used to work for Mr. Cooper. His name's Cade Taylor. Do you know him?"

She groaned when she hung up the phone and noticed the kitchen clock—5:23 a.m. Either Miss Laura must have slept through the phone ringing, or she was already in the barn with a horse emergency. "She'll call me back soon."

Selah shuffled from room to room, clutching the cat. Her mind blank, she studied each pine plank of the floor as she stepped on it. Grandpa's old office was her mom's office now. The room was entirely too cheerful. Mom and Grandma Katie had teamed up to start an online essential oils network. Grandma Katie knew the oils, and Mom did all the monetizing of their site. Once a naysayer, even Selah now always had a bottle of peppermint within easy reach.

But she missed the western horse flavor Grandpa's room used to have. Gone were the pictures of his show horses, his dusty trophy collection, and his stacks of horse training books. She'd personally carried Grandpa's box of knickknack treasures to his truck for his move into Grandma Katie's house at the farm next door. Now the tidy office lacked the comfort she used to find here.

The door to her parents' bedroom was shut. Her dad coughed, and then it was quiet again. He'd get up soon and go on his run before he went to work at the local forest service office.

Normally the memory of the ranger visiting her in the hospital and her talking him into interviewing her dad for a job lifted her heart and brought a victorious smile to her face. That job changed their whole life. But no lift came. Her heart was in such despair—it must be barely beating.

With a sigh, she turned back to the kitchen. She didn't want to be caught downstairs when Dad's alarm went off and the house came alive. Her brothers wouldn't be awake for another hour, but Mom got up with Dad. Selah dreaded the questions about how she was doing. She wasn't doing. In a dazed trance, she continued up the stairs.

The open door to the boys' room lured her near. The floor looked like a Lego dump. Davy's hand hung under the top bunk slat. Michael released his grip on his deep-red, super-soft blanket, and it slipped to the floor. Selah gawked at it knowing it was special to Michael. He might panic if he woke and found it missing. She knew that feeling. She walked to his side and watched his sweet face. Then she eased the blanket under his chin. Michael snorted in his sleep, and she turned like a stiff statue and inched toward her own room.

She plopped onto her window seat cushion and shifted Pearl to her lap. The top of the orange sun torched the bases of the trees lining the pasture. The only thing better than watching the sun come up behind the trees from her room was watching it from Dream's bare back. But today, the light only revealed the emptiness of the pasture and her life. *Please take care of Dream.* She squeezed her eyes shut until her body gave up and slept.

When she woke, her door was ajar. "Pearl?" Her voice an answered echo. "You left me too?" She glared at the crack, but didn't have the strength to get up and close it. She willed herself to go back to sleep so she would feel nothing, but her bladder wouldn't allow it. She unwrapped the ratty old fly sheet, and it slid to the floor behind the door. It had not given her any courage.

In the bathroom, she couldn't look at herself in the mirror. Her blonde hair stuck out in every direction, and she didn't care. Her tongue felt thick as if she'd eaten sawdust gruel. Her eyes flicked to her toothbrush, but she didn't have the energy to go through the motions.

Back in her room, she sat on her bed. Then she flopped to her side and dropped her head on the pillow. While she needed Pearl, it would take more strength than she had to find the cat again.

CHAPTER TEN

EMMA

When she woke, her bed looked like a herd of ponies had galloped through it. Mom was the only one in the kitchen. She sang along with a catchy praise song on the radio. Relief. Whatever upset Mom last night was over. Perhaps the argument wasn't about her horse idea.

"Good morning. Your sister awake?" Seemed like Mom was in an okay mood.

"Yes. She's been in the bathroom for two hours." Brianna was pretty and good at everything. She drew princesses and fairies so real you wanted to touch them. She was the number 2 varsity cheerleader so the popular kids hung out with her. And Mom liked her best because she was perfect. That's not what Brianna said though. *She thinks I get all the attention and always get my own way because I'm deaf. I'd rather be perfect like her.*

"I've been thinking a baby bunny would make a good pet for you." Mom minced onion and tomatoes and slid them into an omelet. "What do you think?" Without waiting for an answer, she chattered on. "A man in our Sunday school class has a litter. I guess that's what you call it. He has six lion-lop bunnies. You can have one if you want it. He showed me pictures." Mom scrolled through the pictures on her phone. "Aren't they the cutest things? I wouldn't mind having a bunny."

"You should get it then, but I want a horse."

Mom's entire demeanor changed. "I should get it? Emma Joy, I hope you were not being rude. I could interpret that comment as rude." One hand braced on the counter and the other on her hip, Mom stared at her.

"Oh no, ma'am. I didn't mean to be rude. Bunnies are darling and all, but I really want a horse."

"It's ridiculous to consider on so many levels. You're only ten."

"I'm old enough to take lessons."

"Taking an occasional lesson is one thing. Being responsible for a horse is quite another." Mom paused and waited for Emma to look at her. "They outweigh you ten times over. They're unpredictable and dangerous." She lifted the edge of the omelet and folded it onto itself.

"My basketball games are more dangerous than a horse. Somebody is always shoving me down," she said.

"I don't think falling to the floor can be compared to falling off a horse."

Emma stood tall. "It's dangerous for Brianna to be at the top of the pyramid of cheerleaders."

"They have to be alert. But she doesn't have a disability either."

"I can't have a horse because I'm deaf?" she signed her outrage.

Mom's eyes locked onto her, and Emma knew she'd better be careful with her words. She slipped into her chair. When she signed again, it was a plea for understanding. "That's so not fair. I'm a good rider."

"I didn't say you weren't. You're at a serious disadvantage already and to add a horse to the equation is not smart. Your riding lessons are in a controlled environment, and they still make me a nervous wreck."

"I've read having a pet helps kids learn to be responsible."

"A bunny or parakeet." Mom slid a wedge of the omelet onto a plate and served it to Emma. "You couldn't do everything for a horse on your own. I have to remind you sometimes to brush your teeth." Mom wagged the spatula at her. "Am I right?"

Emma cringed and nodded. It was true. She forgot things— like taking her shoes off at the door.

"I'm afraid of horses, and they know it. I can't help you look after a horse. I already have enough just taking care of you and Brianna."

Emma's older sister did keep Mom busy. "I'm sure I can do it on my own."

"A horse is expensive. The purchase price is only the start. There's vaccinations *and* farrier bills *and* hay. You're way too young to be responsible for the bills. We have to commit to covering those. On our budget, I don't see a way. Your school is not cheap, and it's our priority."

"I guess I didn't think about all that. Brianna always asks for money so she can go with the squad for football games or for new fancy shoes."

Mom set a bowl of blueberries in front of Emma. "We keep you in basketball shoes too. Girls and their activities are expensive." She kissed Emma's forehead.

"Some of the kids don't want me on the team. They say I play too hard. Like it's important or something. 'It's just a game,' they say. 'Lighten up.' Why play if you're not going to play as hard as you can? I've been thinking I could give up basketball. I won't have time for it anyway when I get a horse."

"No, you couldn't. It's wonderful for you to be on a team."

"It would save a lot of money that I could use to take care of a horse."

Mom tilted her head to the side. Her mouth and eyes were not smiling.

Emma picked at her breakfast. "I saw a flyer in Kim's Feed Store with pictures of horses at an auction. If nobody buys them, they go to Mexico on a big crowded truck and are killed for their meat." Her upper lip rolled in distaste. "We'd be saving a horse's life."

"How could anyone eat a pet?"

Her gaze flicked to Mom's face. Was she considering it? "If I can save five hundred dollars, I can get a good one at auction."

Mom grimaced. She turned her back and slid the cutting board into a pan of soapy water.

After pouring himself a cup of coffee, Dad joined her at the table. Earbuds in, Brianna practically skipped down the stairs. She sang some rap song Emma hated. Since Brianna turned fifteen, she seemed to spend her time working on being even more beautiful. Her blonde hair hung in ringlets from a ponytail positioned near the crown of her head. Her cheeks were pink with blush. Emma's hair was dull compared to Brianna's, and it seemed determined to be straight and limp. It wouldn't hang in a ringlet unless she rinsed it in glue.

Mom poured orange juice for them and sat cradling her mocha. She studied Emma's face. "So a horse is this important?"

"I love them. Horse must have been my first word."

"It wasn't. You were helping your dad plant the garden and your first word was *di–rt*."

Emma glanced at him, but he seemed absorbed in his omelet. She tried to decipher the look on his face. *Hm, he's chewing on a secret.*

Mom swirled her mocha and took a sip. "I want it to go on record I tried to talk you out of it. It's a bad idea every way I look at it." Mom still didn't smile. "Your dad thinks it would be a confidence builder. While I have serious misgiving, your dad and I work together." Mom stared at him when she said, "We've decided to give a horse a try."

Emma forgot to speak and signed. "You mean it?" She flew from her chair, ran past Brianna who seemed absorbed in her own music world, and hugged Mom. "Thank you for giving me a chance. You'll see. It'll be great." When she slammed herself into Dad, she hugged him so tight he peeled her hands off and encouraged her to sit.

"Use your voice, Emma." Before grabbing his keys, he slurped more coffee "Keep saving your money. In six months, or so, when you have enough, we can go see what there is at the auction."

"Six months?"

"Buying a horse is not something to rush into," Mom signed. "But..."

Brianna pulled out one earbud and rubbed her thumb quickly over the tips of her fingers. It wasn't American Sign Language, but she was definitely asking how much money Emma needed. Brianna only knew a few signs. The important ones like—get out of my room, dweeb.

How odd that her sister took time from her own self-absorbed bubble to notice or care what Emma needed. Usually, Brianna acted like she didn't exist. "I need one hundred twenty-five dollars more."

"It would be great to get a horse." Brianna strummed an air-guitar, then wrote a message on a small blackboard. "Saving ten dollars a month for a new guitar. Have ninety dollars." She pointed to Emma with a questioning look.

"Help? That would be amazing." Ownership complications worried her. "Thank you."

"Buy a horse for less. Then you can give it back. Deal?" Brianna wrote.

"I'll pay you back. Every penny." Emma concentrated on forming her words so they'd sound as normal as possible. Brianna would mimic her otherwise. Then Emma turned her full attention to Dad. She grabbed his arm as he headed out the door. "Can we just check out a sale? The flyer said there is one every second Saturday of the month."

"That's in one week," Brianna noted. "Maybe we could come up with more money by then."

"This is moving too fast for me." Mom rose and left the room with her mocha.

"I agree," he said. "We all need time to consider this idea. Not a done deal."

"If we miss the sale this month, it will be a whole month before the next one," Emma argued.

CHAPTER ELEVEN

SELAH

*A*s a soft knock disturbed her sanctuary, she piled the covers up over her head. She couldn't see or talk to anyone. She just couldn't.

The door opened. Her mother whispered, "Selah? School today."

Not moving a muscle, she held her breath. *I can't.* After a couple minutes of quiet, she slipped into a fitful sleep.

Then a dull drumming noise annoyed Selah awake. A small woodpecker with red marks on the side of its head clung to the tree outside her window. She leaned up on one elbow to confirm the unwelcome visitor's identity. Sure enough. He gripped the bark with his toes and slammed his beak into the tree. "You are so rude. I'm sleeping here."

A male cardinal alighted on a branch and blasted its harsh call. "How can you just go on with your day like nothing's happened? Do you see Dream's not here?"

She pictured Dream fighting free of her captor. Maybe the mare would come home on her own. Surely, she wouldn't stop running until she got back to Selah. Weren't there movies about animals finding their own way home? Or even following their families across hundreds of miles to a new home. Those were just movies. That couldn't happen in real life. *I need a miracle.* Selah squeezed her eyes shut and covered her face. After a deep breath, she tried to pray, but there were no words—only blackness.

When the phone rang, she tossed the blanket off her head. "It must be Miss Laura." She struggled to make her feet move faster than a sloth's. Floundering down the stairs, she stumbled into the kitchen like an awkward toddler. "If that's Miss Laura, I'm awake. I'm here."

"Thank you for calling," her mom said, hanging up. Turning, she smiled at Selah. "Good morning. That was your school counselor returning my call. I told him you wouldn't be in school today, but you'd be back tomorrow."

"It's already Monday." Selah sunk back into her tomb of misery.

"I saved you some oatmeal. Hungry?" Without waiting for an answer, her mom slid the pan of oatmeal to the front burner. She bustled around pulling out a bowl and spoon. She brought raisins, pecans, and brown sugar to the kitchen table.

"Did Miss Laura call?"

Mom shook her head and gestured for Selah to sit. "Eat." She set oatmeal in front of her. "I won't take no for an answer."

"I. Can't."

"You must. Before I pick up your brothers from school, I'll swing by the grocery and get some of those little yogurt things in a bottle you like. The boys stay late today for Katie's after-school art class."

Selah curled her upper lip at the lifeless mush in a bowl. After sprinkling the toppings and smothering the gruel with milk, Mom positioned the spoon conveniently as if she was encouraging a little child. She rubbed between Selah's shoulder blades, then sat at the table beside her. After several minutes, the kettle hissed, and Mom rose to make tea. She stood by Selah, balancing a notebook and a teacup. "When you want to talk, you know where to find me." Mom kissed the top of her head and stepped down the hall to the office, leaving Selah to her emptiness.

Lifting the spoon took great effort. She dipped the tip into the oatmeal and brought it to her mouth. It didn't go without her noticing that it was slathered in twice the amount of sugar usually allowed. The sweetness encouraged her to swallow and taste again, but three spoonfuls was all she could manage before her stomach cramped. Her attention shifted to the phone. Why hadn't Miss Laura called her back? Selah dialed her number. Once again, the answering machine picked up. She frowned. Miss Laura had raised Sweet Dream specifically for Selah after Grandma Mary died in a horse accident. Miss Laura would help her find Dream—if only Selah could find Miss Laura. She didn't have any other ideas on who else might help.

Selah trudged to her room and slid her computer from her pack. The best uncle in the world had given it to her for Christmas. The pink-pink cover was perfect for her because it had an apple on it with a bite out of the side. Sweet Dream would have taken that bite.

She plunked cross-legged on her bed and pulled the pillow around to the front, nesting the computer into it. She had to find Miss Laura. Grandpa would have her cell phone number, but with him sick, no way would she bother him. Opening her social media, she searched for Miss Laura's name. After clicking on her profile page, Selah scanned the posts. Three days ago, Laura had posted a video that promised antics of foals learning how to control their long legs. Selah couldn't be bothered to watch that cute stuff now. The next post down was one Miss Laura had shared about a Morgan horse show in Arizona. "Oh no. I bet she went to the show." *Even if I find her, she can't help me.* Selah groaned, closed her computer, curled onto her side, and stared at the texture on her wall. *Oh, please, God. You know where Dream is. Bring her back to me. Are you punishing me? I'm trying to be a better person. I'll help more at home. Anything. Please don't take my Dream.*

Selah became dimly aware of movement downstairs. The chairs in the kitchen scraped, and something heavy crashed to the floor. The muffled voices must be her brothers, home from school already. Soon busy feet charged up the stairs, and Michael burst into her room.

Davy followed. "Michael, you're supposed to be quiet."

"I was quiet." He leapt for the bed and bounced on his knees. "Wasn't I, Selah?"

She sputtered between bounces. "What—are you—doing—home already?"

"Grandma Katie couldn't come teach our art class. Grandpa's still sick."

Selah leaned on an elbow. "He is?"

"Yeah. Dad's gonna get a prescription at the pharmacy."

"What's wrong with him?" she asked.

Davy shrugged. "Blood pressure."

"What's that?" Suddenly weary again, her head dropped onto her pillow.

"Don't know." Davy threw up his hands. "I think it's bad."

Michael stood on his head with his hinny in the air, peering at her.

"Please go away *now*." She closed her eyes. *I can't deal with anything else.* She sensed them withdraw, but a few minutes later, she felt something soft being tucked under her chin and draped over her shoulder. From the musky smell, it had to be Michael's beloved, red plush blanket. He wouldn't part with it long enough to let it go through the washer, but here it was to comfort her. Peeking out of one eye, she watched him tiptoe away.

The next thing she knew, her friend Caroline was talking to her. Disoriented, she sat up. "What are you doing here?"

Caroline's long golden blonde hair had strands from both sides twirled back with purple butterfly clips that perfectly matched her top. The only hint Caroline gave that she was more artistic than perfect was her rebellious, outrageous socks. Today, one was lemon and lime stripped and the other a purple plaid.

"You didn't come to school. I called, and your mom told me what happened."

Selah sniffed and tilted her head from one side to the other to work the kinks in her neck.

"I know." Caroline sat cross-legged beside her on the bed and pulled at a purple yarn on one sock.

"Dream is my whole life." Selah blew her stuffy nose.

"I understand. Besides you, my mare is my best friend. I don't know what I'd do if someone took her."

"Wanted dead or alive—the thief who took my horse!"

"Wonder if Buddy misses her." Caroline scanned the pasture. "Remember fighting off the dogs at old man Tate's farm to rescue him? He was in such terrible shape."

"We couldn't have gotten him home without Dream. So sweet how Dream nickered to him whenever he'd stop and try to lie down. Was a miracle we got him to Katie's farm. A Sweet Dream miracle." Selah sighed. "Grandma Katie loved him back to life."

"And right now, we need another miracle." Caroline grabbed Selah's computer. "What's your password?" She tilted her head back and threw her hands up. "Oh, duh! Sweet Dream." Caroline spent the next half hour searching the web in silence.

Selah lay perfectly still and drifted in and out of sleep.

"Okay. Here we go." Caroline shook her shoulder. "Listen, I'm going to read what they say to do. You have to report her stolen and get a case number. Give them pictures. Especially, close-ups of any identifying markings, including brands and tattoos. Did you do that? It says the first twenty-four hours are critical."

"Yeah! Mr. Cooper called the police and the Texas cattle people. A ranger friend of his came to investigate." Selah peered at the clock. "It's already been two days. And nothing." She glanced at Caroline, then stared out the window. "They haven't found her. She's on her way to Mexico by now."

"Nope. Not gonna happen." Caroline's hands came up together and thrust sharply to the side like an orchestra conductor's downbeat. "No way. No how." Her intensity hardened her face. "Next, it says to make a flyer with her picture on it and put it up everywhere. On telephone poles. In store windows. We could take it to the feed store. Mr. Terry would give it out to all the farriers and ranchers. We should take it to all the vets' offices and—"

"Who will drive us around to all these places?"

Caroline's face contorted as if she were doing a crossword puzzle, her fingers poised over the keyboard. "Good point."

"I can't drive. I don't even have a cell phone. And now somebody took the only thing that's ever been important to me." Selah wrapped a finger in a strand of her hair, twisting it till it knotted. "What a mess."

"You have friends. If anybody stole my mare, you'd be helping. We're going to find her." Caroline gave a quick nod like that settled it. "Amanda just signed onto the internet. Does she know what happened?"

Selah shook her head and sighed.

"I'll message her."

The keyboard clattered for several minutes as Caroline chatted with Amanda. Selah reached for her bottle of peppermint oil hoping to quell the jitters and the familiar sick feeling in her stomach. She scooted the trash can closer to the bed, in case. Rubbing oil on her wrists, she lied down with the scent crushed to her nose.

"Amanda says she's sorry she can't be here to give you a hug in person. She says to remind you she's not the one who moved away. She thinks we need to get busy posting. She'll join Face-Look tonight. She says there are lots of horse groups and tons of sale pages."

"I don't know anybody on Face-Look."

"Grown-ups love it, and Amanda says it's a good way to get the word out. She says to send her a side picture of Dream with her face looking at the camera. Do you have anything like that?"

"On my desktop is a file called precious pictures."

"I see it." Caroline scanned through the pictures until she found what she needed. Then she attached it in an email to Amanda. "I sent it to her and to me. When I get home, I can join some horse groups too and start posting it. I'll have to tell my dad. He let me join Face-Look when I finally turned thirteen because my 4-H has a page. He won't let me be in any other groups. He says the predators troll them. But I'll talk him into it." She searched for horse groups. "It's for a good cause. We have to get the word out. Soon, everyone in the world will hear about Dream. Somebody's got to know something."

For the first time, a surge of hope encouraged Selah. "You think?" She opened her eyes and slowly sat up.

"I'm sure of it." Caroline's fingers flew over the keyboard, but she struggled to talk at the same time. "Amanda said she'll work on making a flyer. She's a wiz. Then she'll email it to us." Caroline flexed her fingers and dived into the keyboard again. "She has an older brother. She thinks, if we pay him, he'll drive her around to put flyers at vet's offices and feed stores."

"That would be great." Selah rolled her stiff shoulders. *I woke up in an old person's body—everything hurts.*

"Have you seen her horse yet? So gorgeous, he takes your breath away. His dapples shimmer in the sunlight." Caroline switched right back to business. "While Amanda makes a flyer, I'm going to focus on putting together a list of the sale barns. They all have websites so my plan is to email them the flyer."

Caroline closed the computer. "I wish I had an uncle like yours. This is an incredible, super-fast computer."

"It'd be better if it had a program that tracked where Dream is."

Caroline rested her elbow on the desk with her chin in one hand while tapping her nose with an index finger. "I know!" After snapping her fingers, she pointed at Selah. "You're the one with connections."

Selah nodded. "You're right. I should post on my blog and all my social media sponsor sites. If I contact all the sponsors who have endorsed Dream and me, the post would spread like wildfire. I've got to pull myself together. I've got to find her now so I'm not sad forever."

"Whoever took Dream isn't going to be able to hide. He's going to wish he'd never met a black mare. We'll find that creep, and we will find Dream—and *he* will be going to jail."

When Caroline got up, Selah untangled her legs and stood. "I'm gonna borrow your optimism until I don't need it anymore."

"Hey. Your sense of humor is back." Caroline gave her a long hug, and they walked downstairs together.

Mom pulled a batch of snicker-doodles from the oven. She grabbed Michael's wrist as his hand shot toward the hot pan. "Any news on Sweet Dream?"

Caroline never took her eyes off the cookies as Mom slid the parchment paper full of cookies to a cooling rack. "Help yourself, girls."

While Selah expressed no interest in the cookies, her brothers tormented each other and battled over the biggest ones. Their cheerfulness was the polar opposite of her despair, but she clung to her thread of hope. Maybe finding Dream wasn't completely impossible.

Caroline smiled as a bite of cookie melted on her tongue. She wiped a stray crumb from her lip, not letting it escape. "We are making a flyer to tell the whole world about Dream and get everyone on the lookout for her."

"That's a great idea. Tag me when you post it, and I can share. My kindergarten homeschooling co-op has a huge following. And my church groups." Mom handed Selah some yogurt. "You need to eat."

Selah's stomach reeled just looking at the yogurt. "I can't. It wouldn't stay down."

Caroline infused her gestures with energy. "We need to get every kid in school to post it on any social media site their parents let them use! And we can get the girls in 4-H and Pony Club to spread the word in their riding clubs."

A vehicle honked outside. "That'd be my dad. Gotta go." Caroline held Selah's arms. "You call me with anything or if you just need to talk. We won't give up. We won't let that evil man get away with this."

Selah's shoulders sagged. "Feels like he's already gotten away with it."

CHAPTER TWELVE

SELAH

Selah lay curled in her bed. Her mind was completely occupied with taking a breath and letting it out to give her aching heart a bit of a rest. She peered through eye slits when Dad knocked and opened the door. *Whoa. When did it get dark outside? How did that happen?* How can empty hours go by so fast when she felt suspended in a time warp? Time was wasting, and she needed ideas for finding Dream.

He sat beside her and rubbed her back. "Mom said Caroline came by."

She mumbled into her pillow. "She's a great friend. Amanda is too."

"I talked to the show director and the police. They don't know anything more, unfortunately. The investigator is concentrating his efforts on finding Cade Taylor."

She rolled over to look at him. "You don't even like Dream."

He gazed out the dark window. "That's kinda beside the point. She belongs to you, and you love her. Do I wish you'd never gotten involved with horses? Every day and in every way." His voice got loud, then quiet again. "Dream's mother killed my mother. And Dream almost killed you."

She tensed. "That's not fair. Dream spooked when lightning hit the tree. Grandma's death was a horrible accident." She sighed with exasperation. "People die in car wrecks every minute."

When he didn't say anything, she reached to touch his arm. "Remember the picture you took of me as a baby? The one with Grandma holding me up to Buddy's nose. I think I learned to walk so I could lead him around." *I was born to love horses. It hurts so much to lose her.*

"You were never leading him. He followed you."

"If Grandma were here—she'd find my horse."

He stood and put one hand up. "Enough. I wanted you to know, I'm keeping in touch with the different departments investigating her disappearance."

She sat upright and spewed some of the anger caged within her. "Theft you mean. Somebody *stole* her."

"Watch yourself, young lady." Dad's mouth tightened. "You need to pretend you're older than thirteen through this. We're doing everything we can to find her. At the very least, keep your outbursts to a minimum."

I want my horse back! Selah yanked the blanket around her. Dad waited while she brought her emotions under control.

She pressed her throbbing temples, then searched in the folds of the sheets for her peppermint oil. She sucked in a deep breath, hoping to quiet her headache, and looked at him, realizing he had more to tell her.

"The police got an address for Cade Taylor and paid his farm a visit." He stepped around puddles of stuff on the floor, one hand on his hip, the other stroking his chin. "Since no one was around, they left a notice taped to the door. A neighbor told the police Taylor's away a lot. They said he keeps to himself and drives a white dually pickup truck just like every other cowboy in Texas. Otherwise, the neighbors don't know much."

"So now they just wait and see if he's nice enough to call them?"

"He's only a person of interest. There's no direct evidence to connect him with the theft."

"Where else can she be?" She started to slide into her hurt when she remembered to ask. "How's Grandpa?"

"Still sick. Katie is fussing over him, but she's worried. If he's not better tomorrow, she wants to drag him back to the doctor. Kicking and screaming if necessary." Dad pulled a wrapped sandwich from his pocket. "Tuna."

Selah dutifully accepted the sandwich and put it on the bed stand.

He slid some books under her bed with his foot and bent to kiss the top of her head. "Get some rest. We'll tackle tomorrow's challenges tomorrow."

She closed her eyes, flopped over in the bed, and sank deeper into the tangled mound of bedcovers. Through the night, she stared at the inside of her eyelids while her mind agonized over the details of the theft. *What if I'd taken Dream to the arena instead of Gringo? What if Grandpa hadn't left? And why isn't Grandpa getting better?* "I'd give anything for a do-over."

On the morning of day three, a puff of air spurted across Selah's cheek. When she opened her eyes, Michael's face was inches from her nose. Her lids dropped shut again. "Leave me alone."

"Selah," his impish voice sing-songed. "It's time for school. Get up—Mom said." His bare feet padded away.

She didn't move. The birds in the tree outside her window twittered spiritedly. Was this the second day or the third? Was it Tuesday? Who cared? The stairs groaned, warning someone was coming. She snugged the covers over her head. Mom lifted the corner of the sheet from Selah's face and sat on the bed. Her scent made Selah want to take a deep breath. Mom smelled like her favorite Joy essential oil blend today. Selah could use a little joy. Her horse coming home would be joy.

"Good morning. It's a new day." Mom worked the blanket off Selah, giving it a little tug where it lay wedged underneath.

"Not a good day."

"I agree it's terrible, but it's not the worst thing. Let's focus on our blessings. Get up now because you're going to school. It doesn't help to find Dream for you to stay curled up on your bed."

Selah started to argue, but Mom flipped the rest of the blankets off. Selah sat up—Mom was right. She needed to fight for Dream. Mom dug through her dresser and tossed her a pair of jeans and the only shirt in her life without a horse on it. "I made your favorite breakfast."

"Can I please stay home? I can't face school yet. I really need to focus on finding Dream."

"It's best. Get dressed and come to breakfast." The look Mom gave her said don't argue.

Selah settled in front of a plate of raisin bread French toast. The warm cinnamon scent was the first food that smelled worth eating in days. Her brothers took turns slurping the last of their juice and dashed for their backpacks. Michael's red and blue superhero pack had nothing in it except a pencil and a stuffed hedgehog. Already to the age where he didn't like Mom taking them to school, Davy challenged Michael. "Race you to the bus." As Michael sped after Davy, the head of his hedgehog peeked from the top of his backpack. A chuckle broke free from her gloom.

She mumbled with food in her mouth. "Do I have to take the bus?"

Mom talked into the dishwasher. "Dad is still here. He can take you."

"Oh, good."

As Dad drove her to school, Selah watched life's normal bustle. "When you see people hurrying around, do you wonder what terrible thing might have just happened in their life?"

"You never know. There are a lot of hurting people, so aim to be kind to everyone. It might be the only good thing that happens to them in their day." Dad parked in front of the school. "I know what you're made of. You can do this."

She didn't see the point of school today. Her eyes flicked toward him, then back out the window wishing she didn't have to get out of the car. Every minute not searching for Dream was a wasted minute, and she'd already lost too much precious time hiding under the covers.

Standing at her locker, she lost track of how long she'd been in the hallway buffeted by the raging river of students. This was not where she needed to be. Her mind made lists of things to do to find her horse. She counted the days on her fingers—Saturday to Sunday to Monday to today. Three days. They'd never been apart so long. *What must Dream think?*

She had an inkling that science was not her first class.

Caroline found Selah staring into the empty classroom. "Spanish. Your first class is Spanish." Caroline grabbed her arm and dragged her along. "Pull yourself together. Are you going to fight back and find Dream or drift along in a fog?"

Selah bristled. "You don't know what it's like. Your horse wasn't stolen."

"No. But my best friend's was. I will not let you give up." Caroline hugged her. "We can't find her by dropping into a coma." She nudged Selah and got her feet moving. "Amanda emailed me the flyer. I printed out a copy for us to go over. Here." Caroline jabbed it toward Selah. "Did you post on your social media and your blog?"

"I tried. I stared at the screen, but I didn't know what to write. I couldn't make my brain work."

"We'll do it together later. I've got to get to math. See you at lunch."

Selah unrolled the flyer and stopped breathing. Her eyes riveted on the picture of Sweet Dream at the farm. Her mouth puckered, and a hot tear leaked onto her cheek. Selah knew that look on the mare's face. *She was asking for a carrot. Where are you, Dream? This is a nightmare, and I must wake up.*

At the end of the longest school day ever, Caroline slipped into the bus seat next to her. She clicked open a green ink pen and wrote notes in neat block print across the flyer. Selah stared out the window, watching the world fly by as if she were in a movie about someone else's life. *How did my perfect life movie turn into a horror show?*

When a nudge didn't bring Selah back to reality, Caroline elbowed her harder.

"Ouch! Oh, thanks, Caroline, I needed that."

"I can't do everything for you. As I was saying, while you so rudely ignored me, I have a couple ideas on headlines that would work."

"I'm doing the best I can. I'm sorry. Thank you for helping me."

"I understand. I really do. But we have to get the word out fast. Dream is depending on you."

Selah tilted her head to rest on the bus window. "I couldn't make it come out right."

"Okay... I'll show you. First, you need a great picture to catch people's eye. This one we sent to Amanda is okay, but I would post a picture of you and Dream in an epic moment." She framed her face with the *L* of her fingers and thumbs. "I know. What about that fantastic one Mr. Classan got during the photo shoot? The one where the buzzard flew over and spooked Dream."

"Of me eating the arena dirt?"

"No, silly. Right before that. Dream was in the up-stride of the canter, your arms were out, and your smile was humongous." Caroline held her arms wide, fingers splayed. "That one."

Selah sighed. "I was so happy. On top of the world."

"When you post it, you need a hook at the top."

"A hook? Say somebody stole my horse? Would everybody look for her?"

"You're getting the idea." Caroline nudged Selah with her elbow. "Think of a line like ... *Half My Heart Stolen* or *ALERT—Reward For My Black Mare*. Something that will grab people, and they will have to read your post."

A warmth crept back into Selah's core. *She's out there—somewhere.*

Inspiration flowing, Caroline chattered away. "People need to like you so they'll care about what happened to you."

"Like me?" Crushing her cheeks with her palms, Selah sputtered.

Caroline tapped her green pen. "Tell them a story about you and Dream. Whatever your favorite moment is with her."

"What if I tell them how I found her and how wild she was? And how now, if I sit out on the deck to read a book, she hangs her head over my arm like she wants me to read to her."

"Yeah. Something super sweet. Folks will slurp that up like a red-berry slush. Then they will want to help, and your post will go viral. And we will find her."

"I always knew you had a great legal mind, but I didn't expect a social media coach."

"You can't just leave finding Dream up to the police and the livestock ranger. They've got nothing. Three days of a cold trail. You post that flyer on your main page and share it to the groups you're in. Join every horse group on your social platform and post-post-post. I'm working on a list of bloggers for you. You got this!"

"I've got this," Selah repeated with growing conviction.

"Amanda's brother will pick me up Saturday and drive me and Amanda around to put up flyers. You can come if you want. But I think you should pound the keys and get the word out on social media."

The bus stopped at the end of Selah's driveway.

"You can do this." Caroline thrust the flyer into her hand.

Selah rested her hand on Caroline's arm and leaned against her. "You're an amazing friend. I don't know what I'd do without you and Amanda."

"That's what friends do. They walk with you, even carry you if they have to, until you can walk on your own."

With a quick nod to Caroline, Selah stepped off the bus. The door slapped shut, and the traffic warning signs clunked against the bus. The motor roared and left her standing in a plume of noxious smoke looking down the dirt trail carved by Dream's hooves. "I'm gonna find you, Dream. I'll never give up."

CHAPTER THIRTEEN

SELAH

*T*he house felt empty when she stepped inside. Happy, playful boy noises drifted from the backyard. *Mom must be sitting outside with them.* She'd be savoring her afternoon cup of flowering jasmine tea. Selah climbed the stairs to her room. The lines in the area rug told her Mom had vacuumed today. Her bed was mounded with the things from the floor. Shoving it all off the bed again, she considered flopping onto her pillow. But the need to find her horse was greater than her need to hibernate.

Instead, she dove into straightening her desk. After plopping her pens into a horse cup, she cleared away the papers. Holding her hands over the keyboard, she wiggled all her fingers, then typed with a mission until she had a list of phrases for her post. *Find Dream, find Dream, find Dream* played in her head.

As she struggled to create a media post from Caroline's notes, the computer trash can filled with deleted drafts. Opening her social media, Selah heaved a sigh and got to work. "I can do this! I must do this." She uploaded the picture Caroline suggested. Dream's black mane, feathered with pink highlights, lifted with the wind. Selah pressed her hands into her face. "I don't have time for tears. I've got to fight for Dream." She sifted through her working drafts selecting her words carefully, then formatted her post.

Reward for my Stolen Dream

Please help find my beautiful black mare. She was taken from her stall on Saturday, at the Houston Horse Expo. I'm the only person she trusts. I need her, and she needs me. We belong together. My heart is broken. Please help us.

"Still reads a little choppy, but it's never going to be perfect." She closed her eyes and hit send to her blog mailing list. "I need one somebody to know where Dream is." The next hour she pasted it in every social horse group she found. Before long, her notification box swelled. People from all over the country offered her sympathy and encouragement.

Just as she was about to run downstairs for a snack, a message lit up. "Hi, Selah. I saw your post about your horse. I might know where she is."

With her hands suddenly so shaky, she could barely type. "Really? Where?"

"You're in Canaan, right? Can you meet me at The Grill on Friday after school?"

She clicked through on the link and scanned his social media profile page. He only had one post, so his profile might be new. Or his parents were overprotective like hers, and he wasn't allowed to post. Or he was cool and did SnapChat instead. The profile picture showed him in a bomber jacket sitting on a motorcycle in front of the high school. He was super cute, even if the picture was blurry.

"Tell me. Where is she?" Her fingers stuttered on the keyboard.

"I'll do a little detective work tomorrow. If you want to know what I find out, I'll be there at 3:30. Gotta go now."

Her dad's voice boomed up the stairs. "Come to dinner, Selah."

"Coming!" She answered with a new lift to her spirit. Then she typed out: "Okay, I'll try." She glanced again at his picture so she would be sure to recognize him at The Grill. His sandy brown hair had a slight wave at the crown of his head, but the sides were cut short. He had an air about him like he knew he was super cool.

As she slipped into her chair beside Davy, she dipped to smell the casserole covered in thick cheese. "Mozzarella pasta, yum."

Michael crawled under the table, then squirmed into his chair. He stood on the seat, grabbed a piece of cheesy pasta perched on the dish lip, and smashed it into his mouth.

Selah closed her eyes and kissed the top of his head. "Michael, you're five. You can sit in a chair."

When Dad came around the corner, Michael turned into an angel.

Mom set a bowl of green beans on the table. "Glad to see your appetite's back, Selah."

Her stomach growled. "I am hungry."

"Me too," Michael said.

"Would you like help?" Selah asked him. He nodded enthusiastically. As she spooned food onto Michael's plate, she eyed Davy. He casually slid his green beans into a napkin tucked by his plate.

"I've started posting about Dream on social media sites," she volunteered. "The police are trying, but they don't have even a lead. It's up to me to find Dream."

"I'm glad the shock has worn off and you're ready to get into the fight now," Mom said.

"That's the Selah we know," Dad added.

"I can't let Dream down. She must be so scared, and I'm never going to stop looking until I find her. And the other two horses. I feel awful for that little girl—don't thieves understand horses are family?"

"All they understand is greed." Dad passed the butter and the salt to Davy. "For your beans. It helps. Selah, how are the responses to your posts?"

"People have been great, and I got tons of comments and shares." It flashed across her mind to tell her parents about the guy who said he'd help. But, before she got the words out, Michael spilled his milk onto her dinner plate smothering her green beans. The right opportunity never seemed to come up again.

"Your homework done?" Mom asked as they cleared the dinner table.

"Not even started. I've been posting in groups since I got home." Her thoughts crashed together like the toy trucks the boys played with. *Tell Mom!* drowned in the racket in her head.

If you do, she won't let you go! roared like Michael's monster truck.

This guy knew something—she had to find out. *I need it to be Friday—now!*

Mom took the platter from her. "Go then. I'll finish up."

The moment passed. "I've got to call Caroline first. I'll do it real fast." She hurried into Mom's office. On the table by the window, Mom had a craft project spread out. The desk had several red folders, which meant taxes. The room smelled like lavender potpourri instead of Grandpa's leather chair and books. Although glad to be living in his old house, she missed those weekends when it was just her and Grandpa.

Caroline's mom answered the phone. "She's not back from her 4-H meeting yet. I'll let her know you called."

"Thanks. Tell her it's important."

Davy chased Michael down the hall with a metal car held high in each hand. She headed the other way skipping steps to her room. Pretty sure the guy was the key to finding Dream, Selah felt she could wait on more posting of the flyer. She should get her homework done.

As she grew sleepy and sleepier, she struggled to finish her English required reading. She moved to the bed and balanced *Robinson Crusoe* on her chest. When she woke, the light was off. Red digits glowed 1:33. Miffed at falling asleep and miffed at Caroline for not calling her back, Selah changed into pajamas. She tugged the covers over her head and fumed. *Why didn't you call me?*

Still wide-awake after thirty minutes, she decided to check her social profile for messages. Hundreds of people had left hearts on her post. She quickly read the well-wishing comments and thanked them with a heart.

She planned to catch a ride home Friday from The Grill with Caroline's dad. But if Caroline didn't come to school that day, there'd be nobody to go with her to meet the guy. Then she'd have to ask Mom for a ride. What if Mom wouldn't let her go?

She had to go. She couldn't let Dream disappear forever.

She reached for her bottle of lavender, dabbed some of the oil onto her hands, and smoothed it on her neck. Inhaling deeply, she repeated the verse that always quieted the noise in her mind. *The Lord is gracious and compassionate, slow to anger and rich in love.* If that didn't work, she'd read more *Robinson Crusoe.*

On day four of Sweet Dream's absence, Selah's tension lifted when Caroline climbed on the bus. As she made her way to the seat, she juggled her backpack.

"Why didn't you call me back?" Selah's eyebrows tightened. "It was important."

"I did!" Caroline dropped her pack on the floor and took her seat. "Your mom said you were asleep."

Selah sighed exasperation. "A guy messaged me. He knows where Dream is."

"For real?"

Her face was so close to Caroline's they breathed the same air. "He's doing some detective work and meeting us at The Grill after school on Friday."

"I can't go. I have a dentist appointment," Caroline squeaked.

Selah huffed. "Can you cancel it?"

"Ah, no. My mom is picking me up from school at three. I have a cavity." Caroline opened her mouth and pointed to a black spot. "Who is this guy anyway?"

A shrug lifted Selah's shoulders. "He goes to high school. He saw my post and said he'd seen her. He's seen Dream!"

"I told you posting on social media would work. What did your folks say?"

"I didn't get to tell them. I thought we'd ride the bus into town and then hitch a ride home with your dad."

"You can't go alone."

"I have to. He knows something about Dream."

"Feels like a bad idea."

"I have to." Selah curled her hands into fists as she insisted. "What could go wrong? I'm meeting him at The Grill, not on a country road. Besides, he's super cute."

"Bad, bad idea." Caroline's long bangs fell into her eyes as she shook her head. "Super cute could still be super creepy. I don't like it."

"It'll be fine. There'll be lots of people at The Grill."

"Maybe Mom and I can pick you up when I'm done at the dentist."

"Thanks. That really helps. Friday is forever away though."

Caroline puffed air into her cheeks and released it in one huff. "I still don't like it."

CHAPTER FOURTEEN

EMMA

It took Emma the whole week to convince Dad they should go to the auction—just to look. She rode in the front seat of the car and tried not to alarm Dad with how excited she was. She barely kept her grin from becoming a toothy smile.

The gravel road got bumpier and dustier when he turned at the large white Auction Barn sign. "We are just going to check out how it works. You cannot buy a horse this trip."

"That would be silly. But I brought my money—in case."

"What? You should have left it at home. This is a trial run—nothing more."

"What if I see the perfect horse?"

"We are not buying a horse today, perfect or otherwise." He parked beside a trailer full of calves. "You can't leave the money in the car. The window in the backseat won't roll all the way to the top."

She stuffed her cash deep into her boots. "I didn't think of that."

"How will you know it's the perfect horse, anyway?"

As she crossed her hands over her heart, she closed her eyes. "It will be like we were meant for each other. He will nicker when he sees me, and I will fall in love."

"You're writing a romance novel." Dad sighed. "Girls and horses. I'm not comfortable with you buying a horse from a sale without somebody along who really knows horses—Mrs. Holmes would help you."

She signed, "She would totally help me. We'll just look today."

The sale yard's dirt parking lot overflowed with trucks and trailers. A horse stomped his hoof on the trailer floorboard as they passed. She followed Dad into the sale barn, peering through the trailers' slats. A yearling whinnied as she passed. "What did you do to deserve ending up here? I'm sorry, little buddy. I hope you find a good home." The pens in front of the auctioneer corralled a group of calves. The auctioneer held a microphone to his mouth. It was loud enough she could make out his singsong sales pitch. The men in the bleachers held up numbers, and the auctioneer called out trying to raise the bid.

Dad stopped to talk to a cowhand, and he pointed into the dark barns. She couldn't hear what he asked, but she guessed Dad didn't want to wander. They walked down the alley, the way the cowhand sent them, directly to the horse pens. The sorry conditions of the stalls and the animals crushed her heart. Boards were tied to posts with twine or twisted wire. Few of them had water buckets, and none had hay. Three pieces of hog wire strapped together formed the front of one stall. She felt as if she was breathing dirt. A layer of grimy silt covered every surface.

"None of these horses look like they'd be worth paying money for."

She gasped and signed with a fury. "Look at the scars on the knees of this poor guy. And what happened to his tail?"

"Use your words," he reminded her. "Is this a young one?"

The chestnut horse latched onto the top board and gulped in air.

"I think so." She spoke deliberately to form her words right. Her speech therapy gave her confidence, but speaking required her to concentrate. "It's so skinny, and part of its eyelid's been ripped off. But I know I shouldn't get a horse that cribs."

"What's cribs?"

"A cribber holds onto things with its teeth and sucks in air. It's a bad habit, and they can teach other horses to do it."

"We won't have any other horses, so that's not a problem. Hope this little guy finds a good home," he said.

She flung imaginary trash toward the wall. "Somebody threw him away like he's used toilet paper. How mean."

"Peoples' situations change. You don't know. Sending him here might be the best they could do for him."

"Maybe they were hoping he'd find a girl to love him. Like me." She repeated, "Like me" in sign, gauging Dad's reaction.

"Not like you. Did you want a young horse?"

"I'm a good rider, but I'm not ready to train horses. So, I'd have to spend money to get it trained."

"Right. That won't work." He pointed to a horse with its head in the back corner. "He looks relaxed."

"He's big. He might have some draft horse in him. His back is cushiony. He'd be way comfortable to ride bareback, but look at his split hooves. No hoof, no horse. I read that somewhere. Plus, he's got a big Roman nose."

"Which is?"

"It's a thick clunky nose. Not very pretty and a conformation fault. Except for his feet, he looks healthy though. If a farrier could help him, I'd take him in a minute. He looks honest."

"Honest? How can a horse be honest?"

"You know—willing, and from their attitude, you can tell if you can trust them."

"Well, from the size of him, he might eat like an elephant." Dad put his arm across her shoulder. "You have learned a lot riding with Mrs. Holmes."

Emma stood a little taller as she walked the aisle. "I've read nearly every horse book in her library." When they passed its stall, a red chestnut pinned its ears. As she backed away, she signed, "Danger. He's not happy. Danger zone."

"Movin' on," Dad said. As they approached the next stall, the horse coughed several times. "Nope on that one."

"Poor old thing. Wonder if it's an allergy. A girl at school has allergies."

"Sounds terrible and might be a big vet bill." He steered her away. They walked the entire length of the barn, looking at one pitiful horse after another.

"I want to take them home, feed them, and love on them." She stopped signing and stared. Was this what love at first sight felt like? A pitch-black mare stood against the back stall wall. Her head bobbed slightly as she slept. "So beautiful. I bet the horse is a girl." She moved closer. "I read mares can be temperamental. I don't want a mare, but if I could get a horse today, I'd want her." Dad urged her to walk on, but her heart wouldn't agree. The mare shifted her weight but took no notice of them. "I want to see her move."

"There's no need." He took her hand. "She looks sick. You know—kinda out of it."

"I'm not sure." Her money, stuffed in her boot, rubbed and cramped her ankle. "There is something about her." Emma dug a carrot cookie from her pocket and extended it as far as she could reach. "Come see me, girl. Want a cookie?" The mare opened her eyes, arched, and stretched her neck. Emma beckoned her, but the horse made no move to approach. "She doesn't trust me."

Dad led Emma by the hand along the row of stalls. She glanced over her shoulder as he ushered her away. For an instant, the mare stared directly at her. Emma's heart stopped. That mare had a story to tell. She didn't belong here. Emma felt it deep in her soul.

The loudspeaker overhead crackled, and a woman announced the barn was closed and the horse sale would begin in ten minutes.

"She's the one, Dad!"

"She is? No. She's not. We can't buy a horse now. Mrs. Holmes needs to shop with you, and we can't put a horse in the back seat of the car."

"I know. It's crazy. But I'm sure." As she clutched his shirt sleeves with both hands, her worry level rose. "My heart says— she's meant for me."

"They want us out of here," he said.

"May I go look at the black mare again? Please. She's my heart horse."

"It was a bad idea to come here tonight. We aren't ready to get a horse now."

A thin, old, bearded man appeared at the end of the row with his raised arm directing them to the sale arena.

"Time to go." Dad latched onto Emma's elbow.

As he dragged her from the barn, she looked back at the mare. *My heart is yours.*

The seating around the sale pen held only a splattering of people. As they passed a table near the doorway, the woman said, "You need a number to bid."

"Oh, we're only here to watch," Dad's gaze wandered the room.

Emma held out her hand. "Just in case. I'll take a number." When the woman looked startled, Emma winced. She must be yelling at her. "Sorry," she muttered. With so much background noise, she had a hard time with volume control. She turned and stood on the first bleacher trying to figure out where the best seat might be.

"You're ten, Emma Joy. You can't take a number," he said to her back.

Emma didn't turn around.

"We aren't buying a horse," he explained to the woman. When the woman insisted, he put his signature on the dotted line where she indicated, claiming the number.

Arms pumping, Emma climbed into the bleachers and chose a seat right in the middle where she'd have a good view of the horses and the auctioneer would have a good view of her. She studied the people—the competition—around her. They all looked pretty much the same. Jeans and boots. T-shirts and ball caps, or long-sleeve cotton shirts and cowboy hats. Two ladies in stylish jeans walked in, pausing for only a moment at the table collecting their numbers. They separated with one sitting close to the auctioneer and the other climbing to a row in front of Emma.

The first several lots for sale were small groups of yearlings. The two ladies seemed to be taking turns raising their numbers. Several of the men raised their numbers until the large lots were declared sold. The same men won the bids on several two-year-olds.

While the waiting pens were reloaded with new lots, buyers milled around the auction floor. The lady in front of her dropped her number. Emma got on her knees under the bench and pinched it free of a squashed popcorn box. She smiled as she handed it back to the lady.

"Oh, thank you. I didn't even notice."

Emma tried to read the lady's lips. She pushed her hearing aid deeper into her ear, hoping to hear the soft-spoken lady better. "Do you have a horse picked out?" *Please don't let it be the black mare.*

"I don't have room for one more horse that people threw away." Her harsh words ran together, making them hard for Emma to understand. "Mostly my friend and I are here to raise the bids so the killer buyers have to pay more and can get fewer of the stock. We didn't have time to see what's in the barn today. If there is something that will work for us, we'll certainly try to outbid them. We train therapy horses."

"Raise the bid?" Emma bit her lip, unsure she understood. "Sounds like a game of cards."

"Poker. A bluffing game." The lady smiled. "Are you here for a horse?"

"Yes. But I'm not sure how this works." Emma's eyes widened to take it all in. "We came to check it out, but I saw a horse—and she's *the one!*"

The lady beamed. "I know the feeling. But you need to be super careful at an auction. Usually, these horses end up here for a good reason. It might be a health issue or a behavior issue or both."

Emma's mind kept drifting to the black mare. "They buy them and kill them?"

"Some do. See the man close to the auctioneer in the brown ball cap? And the man by the stock pen in the blue T-shirt. They're killer buyers. There might be others here, but those two we're familiar with. They want as many animals as they can get for as cheap as possible." As the lady talked, Emma slid onto the bench next to her. "They go for blocks of several horses because most individuals won't bid on those. We do because the more the killer buyers spend, the more it cuts into their profits. Best-case scenario is the killer buyer gets discouraged and gets a real job."

Dad moved down a row onto the bench beside Emma. "Hello," he said to the lady. "I'm Ted. Emma's dad."

"Julie." The lady nodded politely and leaned toward Emma. "Those two..." She tipped her head toward a couple young cowboys in pearl snap shirts. "Are looking for horses they can invest some training into and resell. They're good trainers and make a sincere effort to help the horses. We don't bid against them."

"The mare I found is real pretty. I'm scared they will want her." Emma struggled with her words as she watched them with suspicion. *Julie won't bid against them, but I won't let them take my mare without a fight.* "When will they get to the black mare? Are they selling her last because she's the best?" *I'll never be able to afford her.* Swept up in imagining the worst, she twisted one of her pigtails into a knot.

CHAPTER FIFTEEN

EMMA

*E*mma switched hands to worry the other pigtail. "Why don't they hurry up?"

"The auctioneer will take a break in another thirty minutes," Julie explained. "If they don't bring her out, I can get you into the back. Even though I'm a familiar face around here, we can't stay long. You can show her to me, and I'd be happy to give you my impression. We'll see what we can find out."

It was a long thirty minutes for Emma. Finally, Julie leaned to them. "We have to hurry." She jumped up, and Emma followed like her coattail.

Julie nodded to the woman at the table. Someone asked the woman a question just then, and Emma passed by without being noticed. Dad trailed several steps behind, and when he tried to follow, the woman at the table stopped him. "You can't go back there."

He raised his arm to point. "I'm with…"

"You can't go back there. They're moving stock around, so it's for your own safety."

Emma knew Dad stood watching her so she signed, "Thanks, Daddy. You're the greatest."

Leading the way now, Emma hurried to the end of the row. "She's way down here." She approached so quickly the mare startled, raised her head, and turned to stare at her.

Her hands tucked into her tailored vest pockets, Julie strolled along the front of the stall, peering to see more of the horse. "I can understand why you're interested in her. She looks to be a higher quality horse than normally turns up here. Wonder why she's way back here by herself? And she doesn't seem to care there aren't any horse neighbors." She leaned her body one way and then the other checking the horse out. "Her conformation is really nice. I don't see any blemishes or faults or injuries. When something looks too good to be true, you can be sure it is. Likely, the reason her family dumped her is behavior issues."

Julie planted herself squarely in front of the stall and sucked in air between her teeth, making her sound like a finch. Emma cringed at the squeal in her hearing aid, but the horse tilted her head and took one step forward. "From the look in her eyes, either she has a very quiet nature, or she's got drugs in her system."

Emma offered the horse a cookie.

This time the mare extended her nose to sniff. Her lips smacked, but she seemed reluctant to come any closer.

Emma encouraged the horse with a kissing sound. "Or maybe someone's hurt her."

Then, with a quick motion, the mare's teeth snatched the carrot cookie from Emma's hand.

"Not a very respectful gesture on her part." Julie frowned. "Hum. For me, she's worth taking a chance on. But for you, I've no idea what your level of experience is. She might be a challenge. And I'd still want to see her trot. She might be dead lame for all we know."

Emma didn't catch everything Julie said, but she heard enough to get the idea. "She's scared. Aren't you, pretty girl?" Emma spoke as if to comfort a baby. The mare stretched her nose toward Emma again. "She likes me." Emma reached through the rails and put her hands on either side of the horse's face. As they gazed into each other's eyes, a small seed of trust sprouted between them. The mare's nostrils flared. When Emma eased her face closer, the mare sniffed her skin. She rested her cheek on the mare's velvet muzzle. Then she turned to Julie. "I think she loves me. She needs me to get her out of here."

The overhead speaker crackled, and the auctioneer's voice called in the next sale lot.

"She does seem to be taken with you. If the horse is rideable, they'll have someone ride it during the bidding. Let's get back."

"Isn't she the most beautiful, amazing thing ever?"

"Don't let beauty dazzle you. Her temperament is the greater concern. Beauty can camouflage a mean spirit." Julie moved briskly so Emma jogged to catch her.

Emma found her dad right where she'd left him. She grabbed his arm and tugged him to follow them to their seats. "She's great, Dad. I feel it here." Emma put her fist over her heart. "The lady says they will probably ride her, and if she does good, can I bid on her? Please? The lady thinks she's good too. She said a higher quality than most that go through here. Please?"

"We aren't prepared to buy a horse today." He scratched his head. "I'm being sucked into a vortex. If it doesn't kill me, your mother will."

"But if she's the one…" Emma leaned into him.

The two cowboys held up their number to bid on a young Paint horse.

"I have a bid of three hundred. Do I see, three twenty-five? This is a solid horse, folks. Young and unspoiled. Three ten? Going, going, gone to number 17 for three hundred."

The killer buyers waited together on the side wall as the cowboys picked up two more sorrel geldings. They walked to the table with their number and cashed out.

"They're done?" Her squeal of delight caused people to turn and stare. "Oops, too loud." She clamped her hand over her mouth.

Julie whispered, "Looks like it, but they aren't the last of your competition. See the man who walked in? He has a dude ranch and looks for horses with loud coloring—a Paint horse or an Appaloosa. A lovely black mare would suit him. Several people in the room haven't bid on anything yet. How much were you wanting to spend?"

"I have four hundred sixty-five dollars."

Attendants swung the gates open, and a wrangler rode the roman-nosed gelding into the arena. He trotted one full circle, and the auctioneer started the bidding. "What will you give for a ten-year-old horse with a good disposition? He loads and stands for the farrier. I'm sure he's got draft horse bloodlines, so he can pull a wagon or logs if you need him to. Don't let that nose hold you back, folks. This is a good boy. Let the bidding start at two hundred."

One of the killer buyers stepped forward and raised his number high.

"Oh no, you don't." Julie sat perfectly still watching. "They need to pick 'em up cheap or lose money. That big red horse is probably almost fifteen hundred pounds. Last I checked, the killers can get forty cents a pound or around six hundred dollars."

Someone else bid, and the killer countered. Just as it looked like he would take the horse, Julie's partner raised her number and jumped in.

The auctioneer pointed at the killer buyer. "Will you give me four seventy-five?" As he tossed his cigarette into the dirt, grinding it out with his boot heel, the killer buyer put up his hand like a stop sign.

In her excitement, Emma threw up her hands to cheer and knocked her hearing aid loose.

"Yes," Julie said. "Saved one. He'll make a nice therapy horse."

"What?" Emma snatched the aid before it fell through the bleachers. She tucked and wiggled it back into her ear.

"You use a hearing aid?"

"Only in one ear. I'm totally deaf in the other."

"Oh my. I'm sorry. Is it safe for you to be around horses then? You need all your senses to be aware of what they're doing."

Emma's mouth dried out as she feared the lady would stop advising her. "I take lessons and do great."

Julie cast a glance at Dad. He nodded. "She does fine. We believe deaf children can do anything they've a mind to do. Especially this one." He gave a quick nod in Emma's direction as he teased her. "With one exception, I should add. You won't be buying a horse today. Not even a pretty black one."

In the meantime, they auctioned two more horses, and Emma grew anxious to see the mare.

His phone buzzed. "Your mother," he said. "Be right back."

Peering into the darkness of the barn, Emma spotted the black horse walking calmly toward her new life. Did the pretty horse know how much trouble she was in? Anything could happen. The man wearing roweled spurs the size of silver dollars might buy her. Or she could spend her days at the dude ranch with kids kicking her belly and snatching the bit in her mouth. Or worst of all, the killers could get her. She couldn't let that happen. Emma bit the inside of her cheek, and her legs jiggled on the wooden bleacher. *I've got to save her.*

The announcer talked her up. "This is the horse you've been waiting for. What a beauty. She's kid broke. Six-years-old. Trailers, stands for clipping, and is perfect for the farrier. Safe for anyone. Trail trained. Use her English or Western."

The killer buyer moved into the auctioneer's line of sight with his number ready.

"I'd hate to see him get her." Julie sighed. "Because of her quality, he'll bid higher."

Emma alerted. "The killer buyer wants her."

"Looks that way. Though he wouldn't actually put her on the truck to the slaughterhouse. He'd post her for sale claiming she'd be killed unless someone rescued her. He'd pile on the pressure with a two-day deadline. He'd end up selling her for at least twice what he paid. Then he'd be able to buy three or four other horses that he *would* put on the truck. It's an ugly racket."

"Horrible." Emma covered her open mouth.

"I know. I wish it was possible to save them all."

The auctioneer swung his finger around the room at the crowd. "Folks, this is an exceptional mare we've got right here. Look at her conformation. You could raise high-quality babies out of her. Let the bidding start at three hundred."

Emma intently watched the killer buyer. She gripped her bidding number card.

"Your dad said you weren't buying a horse today." Julie patted Emma's hand.

"This mare is for someone special. Is that you, mister?" The auctioneer pointed to a man who shook his head. The killer buyer stuck his number card high.

Emma looked anxiously at Julie, who rested her hand over Emma's hand still gripping the number.

The dude ranch owner raised the bid to three hundred fifty only to be outbid by someone behind Emma.

The wrangler hopped onto the horse bareback. With only a halter, he walked and trotted the mare around the small arena.

"Not lame." Julie noted right away. "That makes her being here an even bigger mystery."

The mare's head was low, and she ignored the activity in the room. When he pivoted her, using only his legs and the rope tied to her halter, she jog-trotted in the other direction.

Emma signed, then whispered, "Quiet as a lamb."

Julie agreed. "And very well trained. Soft and responsive, but something is nagging at me. Her eyes look dull, and she seems a bit sluggish. That screams drugged to me."

The rider slung a strap tied to his wrist from one side of the horse to the other. It slapped her shoulder, urging her to canter. The horse's ears flattened.

"Uh-oh," Julie said.

When the mare refused to canter, the rider dug his spurs into her side.

Wide-eyed, Emma watched as the horse snaked her head around, twisting her body into a donut shape. She snatched the wrangler's pant leg in her teeth, yanked him from her back, and dumped him unceremoniously into the dirt. *Wow. You taught him a lesson!*

Julie leaned to Emma. "Never in all my years have I seen a dismount like that one. Glad you weren't bidding on her."

When dad finished his call with Mom, he returned and took his seat beside Emma. "Did you see that? Stay away from that beast."

The stunned auctioneer found his voice. "That's okay, folks. The mare has spunk. She'll make a great horse for the right person. I've got three fifty—do I hear four?" He pressured the previous bidders one at a time, and each shook their head no.

Even though Emma didn't want to bring attention to herself in a room full of strangers, she couldn't stand it anymore. When the killer buyer started to raise his number, her hand darted skyward, holding her number card high.

Julie spoke sharply. "Not a good idea."

The auctioneer was instantly on her bid. "Four hundred to the cute little girl in pigtails. All right, folks, you gonna give this mare up or give me four twenty-five?"

"Emma Joy!" Dad tagged on her middle name. "What possessed you to bid on that horse? You saw how she acted."

"I couldn't let the killers get her."

Dad asked Julie, "I know nothing about horses. What do you think? To me, she seemed mean just then."

Julie turned slightly to talk to him. "She has some serious attitude, and I wouldn't advise her for a child. You have to wait for someone to outbid you at this point."

"I've got a wrangler who will fix her, I'll bid four twenty-five," rang clear from the back.

Julie smiled, nodded at Dad, and relaxed with a sigh.

Emma spun around. "What did he say?"

"It's for the best, Emma." He reached for her hand. "A man in the back outbid you. You have to let it go. She needs an experienced horse wrangler person."

"Folks, don't let this special mare get away." His auctioneer singsong started again. "She's a bargain at twice the price. Look at the way she's put together. She just needs someone who understands her. I've got four twenty-five. Anyone give me four fifty? She's worth every dime."

I understand her! Her hand shot high, waving her lucky number before her dad knew it. Julie grabbed it and pulled it down. This time the auctioneer missed her bid. Dad growled as he pried the number stick from her hand.

The gavel slammed, and "Sold for four twenty-five" echoed against the metal walls.

A sadness crushed her. She'd lost. What would happen to the mare?

Emma stood. When she walked down the bleacher steps toward the horse, she felt the horse's dark eyes following her. Her heart apologized, and she bit her lip, refusing to cry.

I'm so sorry. I wanted us to be together. Emma reached her fingers toward the mare while the horse's nose stretched toward her. *Feels like velvet.* Her arm draped around the horse's neck, and her nose buried in its mane.

A hush fell over the room as if everyone marveled at the connection and tenderness between them. The announcer coughed, then sniffed. "Folks, we have a problem. My mamma always said love is more important than anything. This here is love." He addressed the high bidder. "Sir, you won the bid on the horse. It's your call."

"I'm a grandpa. If I kept those two apart, I couldn't sleep tonight. I withdraw my bid. Give that mare to Pigtails."

Some in the crowd clapped.

Emma choked on emotion and hugged the mare. With her eyes full of grateful tears, she waved at the people in the room. She threw off her shyness, ran toward the man in the big white hat, and hugged him like he was her own grandpa.

After a few moments, he waved his Stetson in the direction of the horse. "Go get your mare, young lady."

As the gavel fell, she turned to the announcer. "Sold to Pigtails."

Sold to me!

"Step to the table and claim your new horse."

Jumping up and down, Emma raised both fists high. Then she scrambled from the bleachers to the sale table.

Dad got to the table first. "I appreciate everyone's kindness, but this is a big mistake. She's a child, and she didn't understand."

"Is this your signature, sir?"

He nodded. "But—"

"Sorry, bubba, sales are final."

Julie tried to help. "The girl is deaf. You can't sell a horse with a mean streak to her."

Indignant, Emma pulled her shoulders back. "She's not mean. She's scared. Is there a law that says deaf people can't have horses? She's mine." She pointed to the black mare standing nearby.

While the wrangler seemed none too worse from the dumping episode, he stood at the very end of the lead rope. The horse held her head high, her neck stiff, and her eyes fixed on him.

Dad wiped his hand down his face and blew air loudly from his mouth. "Oh, Emma. What have you done?"

Emma bent and dug her cache from her boot. She laid it out before the cashier to become the proud owner of the beautiful velvety horse with a sketchy past.

CHAPTER SIXTEEN

SELAH

Selah checked out every table in The Grill, but didn't see the guy. She found a booth where she could watch the door and ordered a chocolate milkshake. Since she hadn't even been able to look at food, she'd skipped lunch. But the milkshake tasted smooth and amazing. There were a couple familiar faces around the room, but she couldn't put a name with any of them. They probably all knew Grandpa. She shook off the chill from realizing she was meeting with a high school guy she didn't know, even if he was cute. She hoped he wasn't pranking her. Where was he anyway? The clock over the door showed ten to four. *Didn't he say three thirty? Maybe he didn't really know anything, and that's why he wasn't here.*

Then a man strode toward her. His jeans needed washing, and his striped pullover was equally shapeless. His slip-on shoes were like the soft-sided ones Grandpa wore when his feet hurt. Smiling, he dropped into the bench seat across from her. "Selah, right?"

She nodded, too shocked to speak. *This can't be him. No way is this guy in high school.*

He didn't look at all like his picture. His jaw was square and his neck thick. His huge forehead had one clump of hair with a touch of gray right in the middle.

She bit the inside of her cheek. As she swirled the straw in her shake, she wondered if she should bolt for the door. *I have to find out what he knows about Dream.* She took a casual sip of her shake, disguising her rising concern. "Who are you?"

"Chip. As in chip off the old block."

Where had he come from? Not the front door. Strange. Had he been in the bathroom all this time? He smelled stale, like a cup of coffee after Grandpa left it in the barn. *He seems kinda creepy, but he can help me. He's all I've got.* "You look different in person."

"I haven't updated my profile picture in a while. I see you have a drink. Can I get you a pastry?"

"No, but thanks. I figured you were in high school?" He was probably trying to look charming as he smiled and shrugged. She suppressed a shiver.

"I put your name into a search engine and found a link to a training video you made at Cooper's Center. You're a talented rider."

"Thanks." *He likes horses.* She relaxed her guard. "My horse is amazing."

"I love horses, and I was sad to hear somebody stole her." He shook his head no as the waitress approached the table. "Who would do a thing like that?"

"A horrible person. You said you might have seen her."

"It's sad. Did you raise her from a foal?"

"No. My grandma died when I was four, and her best friend raised Sweet Dream just for me."

"Wow. So she's not just any ole horse to you?"

"She's everything to me." Her thoughts turned inward, and her mind drifted.

"From the picture you posted, she looks like a nice horse." He stared into her eyes, looking intent and interested. "I'm sure she will turn up."

"You said you've seen her. Where?"

"I thought so, but I found out the horse that looked like yours is owned by an older lady. She's had it for years." He smiled slightly, reflecting sympathy. "Sorry to get your hopes up. I'll keep looking though."

"I'm sorry too." Selah pushed her milkshake away.

"You'll find her. I feel bad my lead didn't pan out," he said.

She propped her chin in her hand and stared at the sugar packets.

"Say. I have a couple of preview movie tickets. It's about a two-year-old racing filly that was beating all the colts until she broke her foreleg. It's tragic, but a great story."

"*Ruffian*? You have tickets to *Ruffian*?" She studied Chip with new interest. "Wow. I'd like to see that."

"It might distract you for a little while. It's less than two hours." He leaned his elbows on the table and smiled. "You're a sweet girl, and I'd really like to do something nice for you. It starts in about fifteen minutes. Come on. It'll cheer you up. What do ya say?"

"I can't, thanks." She shook her head. "My friend is picking me up after her dental appointment." She flipped her notebook closed. Her neck felt prickly. What had Mom always told her about listening to her spirit? A chill rushed through her body, and in her heart, she knew it was a warning. She stuffed the notebook in her pack, and her hands shook as she fumbled to zip it. She had to get away. Deciding to walk to the dentist office a couple blocks away, she stood and slung the pack over her shoulder. As she headed for the door, he got up and strolled along with her.

"I'm sorry I wasn't much help finding your horse. I sure hope she turns up. You know how to contact me so let me know how it's going."

As her fear level rose, her thoughts became crystal clear—she shouldn't step outside with this guy. She spun to the nearest booth where two men with plumbing company patches on their shirts ate burgers. "I need help," she said.

At that moment, Caroline's mom threw open the door and thundered into The Grill. "Who do you think you are?" she demanded of him.

"Take it easy, lady." Chip faced her.

Selah's head jerked from Caroline's mom to the guy and back again with her eyes wide and her heart beating like a trapped sparrow.

The two men stood, one on either side of her. The people in The Grill stopped eating and gaped. The stranger pivoted on his heel and, in a flash, hurried out the door. The men chased him.

"What were you thinking, Selah?" Caroline's mom panted as if she'd been running. "When Caroline asked me about giving you a ride home, I couldn't believe you'd meet someone off the internet. How could you fall for a trick like this?"

"I know. I feel so bad." Selah's lips trembled as quick breaths spurted in and out. *He wanted to hurt me.* She stepped toward a chair, but her legs locked. Someone handed her a glass of water, but it sloshed violently when she tried to take a sip. Caroline's mom grabbed Selah's elbow as her knees threatened to buckle. She gulped. "You gonna tell my mom?"

"You bet."

The men returned to the restaurant. "Sorry. We lost him. He took off in a white van." They went back to their lunch.

"Do you have any idea how much danger you put yourself in?" Caroline's mom's voice carried through The Grill, and everyone pretended not to watch. This didn't happen in Canaan. "Get in the car." She pulled Selah by the arm and hauled her outside The Grill where evil had been prowling only a moment before.

The lump in Selah's throat refused to go down. *My only lead on Dream turned out to be a creep.*

Caroline's mom didn't say a single word as she drove Selah home. Caroline and Selah sat stiffly in the back seat equally quiet. As their eyes met, they grimaced. When the car stopped in front of Selah's house, Caroline's mom thrust it into park and slammed the door shut after she got out.

Neither girl wanted to move. "I told you this was a bad idea," Caroline muttered.

In slow motion, Selah eased out of the car and held her hand up in a wave to Caroline. Caroline's mother entered the house without knocking and called loudly. "Karen!"

Selah's mom rushed to her friend. Grasping her sleeve, she gave Caroline's mom her complete attention.

"A man off the internet got Selah to meet him at The Grill."

Mom's mouth dropped open. Her fingertips together, she covered her nose and mouth and closed her eyes. "No!" When her eyes opened and met Selah's, she screamed, "What were you thinking!"

"I thought…I thought he was my chance to find Dream."

CHAPTER SEVENTEEN

EMMA

Emma led her new horse to a grassy area outside the auction house to allow it to graze while they waited for Mrs. Holmes. The horse ate quietly, but Emma couldn't stand still. She bounced on her toes. How lucky that Mrs. Holmes had answered her phone and agreed to come transport her equine treasure. She would've walked the horse the sixty miles along the highway if she had to. Maybe it was "rash" like Dad said. But what else could she do? It was meant to be. This was her horse.

Hands on his hips, Dad paced in the parking lot—probably trying to figure out what to tell Mom. Hopefully, Mrs. Holmes would say the horse was perfect and a bargain.

Since Emma had to match the winning bid of the nice grandpa, she only had forty dollars left. She planned to save for a saddle and pad, a pink halter, a bridle, body-brushes, a hoof pick, and she'd need a feed bucket. She'd have to start making slime right away, and she made a mental list of other things she could do to earn money. Of course, it was only right that she pay her sister back first.

Mrs. Holmes's brownish gold pickup truck turned into the sale lot and parked alongside the grassy area. She slid out and waved to Dad as she walked to meet the new horse. "Nice." She put out her hand for the lead rope. "Can I see what you've got?" She drew the horse away from the grass and led her to a dirt area. She kept the mare's head tipped toward her as she ran her hands over its body. "So far so good." Mrs. Holmes opened the mare's mouth to check her teeth. "Not that old. In the five-to-eight range." She handed the lead rope back and lifted each hoof. "From the overall look of her, I'd say she's a Morgan. And you got her for four twenty-five? Amazing considering her quality."

"My heart said she was the one for me."

"She knows what's expected of her. She's obviously well trained. I'm confused about why she'd be drugged."

Dad smirked. "Not so confusing, really. She deliberately reached around and jerked the wrangler off her back."

"No way." Mrs. Holmes spurted a high-pitched laugh that escalated into a coughing fit. As she pounded her chest with her fist, she blew out a couple exaggerated breaths until she regained her composure. She flicked the light from her phone across the horse's eye. "Let's take a look. A vet would tell you for sure, but her pupil is hardly reactive. It's a good guess she's drugged."

"Why?"

"She might have pain somewhere, or she was too hard for the seller to handle."

Dad scraped his fingers up the sides of his head and interlaced them on top. "I don't like the sounds of that."

Mrs. Holmes grimaced. "It's worrisome but pretty typical for horses coming out of the sale barns. If she turns out to be a horror, we can bring her back and resell her."

"She should get a chance!" Palms together as if praying, Emma moved her hands toward Dad and back signing a plea for the horse.

One arm around Emma, Mrs. Holmes gave her a quick hug. "She will get a chance. Shall we take her home?"

Emma relaxed and nodded.

"Open the trailer door and drop the ramp. This is the real test. Can we get her in?" Mrs. Holmes took the lead rope and led the mare toward the trailer.

Six feet from the door, a brightness came to the mare's eyes. The horse halted and stepped backward.

Mrs. Holmes pivoted to face the horse and made her back ten more steps. Then she turned around and attempted to walk casually toward the trailer.

The mare shook her black head violently, trying to get free. When that didn't work, she arched her neck and reared. The moment her front feet hit the ground, she scrambled backward, scattering small rocks in every direction.

"Whatever level of drugs she still has in her system won't keep her quiet enough to load her. We need help," Mrs. Holmes said.

"I'll go ask." Emma sprinted to the barn.

Dad groaned.

Four stout men followed her to the trailer. One took the lead rope from Mrs. Holmes. Two others ran a hefty butt-rope behind and under the horse's tail. The fourth carried a long pole whip.

Emma watched horrified, her hand clamped over her mouth to keep her from screaming. But if she interfered, the horse wouldn't be coming home.

The first man jerked on her halter. "Gotta show her who's boss."

The mare responded by rearing and pawing the air with her hooves.

The two men on the butt-rope leaned toward the trailer, applying pressure. The third man smacked her hip with the whip.

Emma gulped, sure the mare snarled. One hind leg struck at the men behind her. Together they hauled her a few steps closer to the trailer. Squealing as she reared, the horse resisted the pressure of the butt-rope and thrashed like an enraged demon.

A fifth man came running. He moved with great caution to her head and threw a cloth bonnet over her ears and eyes. He jumped away as she slashed at him with a front hoof.

"Holy cow!" Dad exclaimed. "Forget it. Leave that beast here."

In the next moment, the group of men heaved the horse onto the trailer and secured the door. "You can keep the blindfold," one of them said as they left.

Mrs. Holmes swallowed hard. "I don't know what to say."

"When she gets to know me, it will be all right." *I hope.* "Can we take the blindfold off now?"

"She's quiet, so let's leave it." Mrs. Holmes peered into the trailer. "Well, let's go home." She suggested tentatively. "Want to ride with me, Emma? You can tell me about the auction."

"Can I?" she pleaded to Dad.

"Yes. You should." His hair was disheveled like a squirrel ran through it. "I need time to figure out how to explain this to your mother. I've got to call her and prepare her, the best I can, for what we've done. We might be sleeping in the lawn mower shed this week."

"Oh, Daddy. I will work with the mare. Mom will see how beautiful she is and fall in love. She'll be chopping carrots and hanging out at the pasture fence. You'll see."

"I doubt it. Some fears are too deep."

Mrs. Holmes started the truck. "There are snacks in the glove box. And water behind the seat. Why is your mom so anxious about horses?"

"Her best friend in high school had horses and was a good rider. But she was killed when her horse spooked. She fell and hit her head on a wheelbarrow."

"Tragic. A helmet might have saved her life. No wonder your mom is so protective of you."

Emma unwrapped a chocolate bar and waved it under her nose. "I can't think of anything as good as chocolate except your own horse."

"Chocolate is like joy that melts in your mouth. Hand me one, please."

Emma giggled and dug through the box "Do you think that, because they used drugs on her, the mare is not acting herself?"

"I'm afraid we're likely to see much worse. We'll know for sure when it wears off. At least she is riding quietly back there and not tearing up my trailer." The truck picked up speed, and they got on the highway. "In the meantime, stay away from her. I'm afraid for you. If we get her in your pasture, be especially watchful. Don't take any chances."

"But... we waited for over an hour for you. That whole time she was sweet as pie. She ate grass next to the parking lot and acted like a lamb. She acted like a completely different horse from the one those scary men threw into the trailer." Emma stared at the taillights on Dad's car. "I figured out what it is! She's afraid of trailers."

"That's possible."

"The other bad things she did were because those men were hurting her."

"True. You might be on to something. Not all horses will put up with abuse. Most will react with fear, but some will fight back. You've got a fighter."

When Mrs. Holmes parked in front of Emma's house, Mom waited on the porch with her arms crossed. Balanced on her toes, Brianna rocked the swing and barely looked up from her phone. Emma crossed two fingers of both hands and held them over her lips.

Then she leaped from the truck and ran to the trailer to check on her horse. "She got the blindfold off." The mare slung one foot like it was a fly swatter and slapped it on the floor of the trailer. Bam. Bam. Bam.

One hand on the horse, Mrs. Holmes talked soothingly and swung the butt bar out of the way with the other. Without taking her eyes off the trembling horse, she rubbed small circles on her hindquarters as she moved into position to grab the dangling lead rope. The mare stopped slamming her hoof, and her ears pivoted to Mrs. Holmes.

Emma ran to her dad's car. "I know what was wrong. She was defending herself from those men. And she's afraid of trailers. Please, give her a chance." Dashing back to the trailer, she held her breath and watched Mrs. Holmes.

When the trainer backed the horse out, Emma's sister brightened and squealed, "She's dreamy." Brianna snapped and posted a picture on SnapChat. "Can I pet her? Can I take a selfie with her?"

"May I," Dad muttered. "No and no. You can't get anywhere near her until we know her better."

Emma pointed to the horse. "She's in a brand-new place, and all she's doing is looking around."

Dad walked to the porch where Mom waited. Emma's hair stood up on her arms like a lightning storm was near. Did she hear thunder? She could have sworn so.

When Emma reached out to take the lead rope, Mrs. Holmes hesitated. "Can you handle her okay?"

"She'll be great." Emma walked away confidently, and the horse followed like a pup.

Mrs. Holmes shut the trailer door. "I'll watch to see how it goes."

As Dad called, he leapt from the porch toward Emma to get her attention. "Mrs. Holmes should put her in the pasture," he signed emphatically.

"I'm being careful. I'll keep her as far away from me as I can. Even if she acts silly, which she won't, I will stay out of the way. I got this, Dad. No worries."

Even though she thanked Mrs. Holmes over and over, more gratitude bubbled up. "I would have led her all the way home, but I'm glad I didn't have to. Thank you."

"Ha. Sixty miles is a long walk."

As Emma brought the horse to the porch, the muscles in Mom's face never moved, and a bit of red tinged Dad's face. As the mare dropped her head to graze in the front yard, Mom stared at the horse. She lowered her chin, glared at Dad, then shook her head and went inside.

Keeping a safe distance away, Brianna circled around the horse exclaiming her wonder. "I can't wait to ride her. I'm so excited to be a part-owner of a horse."

Emma considered telling her sister she was paying her back, then bit her tongue. For now, having another ally in the family was best. As soon as Brianna had a new boyfriend, she'd forget about the horse anyway.

"Guess, you picked up on the fact your mother is not happy," Dad signed. "Go introduce this black surprise to her new pasture, then come in and talk to your mom."

Emma's mouth puckered, but she resolved not to be upset on the happiest day of her whole life. Her hand slipped under the horse's mane. She never wanted to stop rubbing her fingers through the mare's soft winter coat. "Don't you worry." She led the horse past the garden shed into the backyard.

Brianna swung open the gate to the small pasture, and Emma swelled with happiness and pride leading her amazing horse.

At the pasture gate, Emma waved an enthusiastic all clear to Mrs. Holmes. She walked the horse along the pasture's fence line. "Now you know where the fence is. Don't get scared and run into it and hurt yourself. I can't afford a vet." Emma kissed the mare's nose. "We'll be great friends." Undoing the halter, she released the horse and stepped away in case she kicked out.

The mare paused a moment, then gave a weak whinny before trotting to the nearest fence and staring off into the distance.

While Brianna snapped pictures and posted them with lightning speed, Dad heaved a big bucket over the fence and unrolled a water hose. "How's she doing?" he called.

Emma answered with a thumbs-up and a smile. Amazingly, Brianna ran to pull the hose through the fence and held it in the bucket. If her cheerleader friends could see her now.

The three of them clustered around the water bucket, marveling at the new toy that moved. Emma thought of Mom and glanced toward the house in time to see her step back from the window.

"Does she need anything besides water? Hay or horse food?"

"There's plenty of grass. That's all she needs."

"Let's go face the music," Dad said.

"I'll stay and watch her," Brianna volunteered.

Emma made what she hoped was a recognizable chicken noise at Brianna and straggled after Dad. *Even if I sound like a frog, Brianna will know what I mean.* As they headed to the house, Emma tried to figure out her best defense. But the truth was the best way through.

Remembering to kick her shoes off at the door, she stepped into the kitchen. Mom stood stirring a pot on the stove with her back to Emma. Dad poured sweet tea and settled in at the kitchen table.

Emma spoke quietly. "A lady at the sale helped me. She comes all the time to save horses from killer buyers. She said this mare was a quality horse."

Mom stirred the pot. Dad moved only his eyes between them.

"There was something about her. She is special. She didn't belong there."

Mom kept stirring the pot.

"You've always told me to listen to my heart. My heart told me she was the horse for me." Emma's shy, confident smile expressed her heart. The horse was amazing, and she could hardly believe she was the owner. All those basketball games where she learned to be tough and aggressive paid off—she had a horse to prove it.

Mom put down the spoon. Her chest rose and then fell with an exhale. She zeroed in on Dad's face. "And you approve? We talked about this. You know the problems. I trusted you...."

Dad stood in front of Mom. His hands on her arms, he rubbed gently. "I know. You're right. I admit I wish I hadn't taken her to the auction. I was bamboozled. But Emma's smitten with this horse." When Mom looked away, he dipped his head to catch her gaze. "I'm sorry. But at this point, I'm okay with taking the horse on trial. One good thing I see is I won't have to mow so much."

In spite of the kitchen heat, Mom crossed her arms as if she was cold. She stepped back from Dad. "And what's the plan if she doesn't work out?"

"We can resell her at the same sale barn."

Emma tensed, but it was a good time to be quiet.

Mom fixed her eyes on her daughter. "A horse is a lot of responsibility. I'll not be reminding you to take care of it."

"You'll see, Mom. She's great. I'll take care of her. You said a pet would help me learn to be more responsible."

"It might be working already. I see you remembered to take your shoes off."

Emma smiled, but Mom didn't.

"If I get even an inkling this horse is dangerous in any way— she goes."

"Yes, ma'am."

Mom stared intently at Dad. "Neither of you may leave the house together—ever again. I'm afraid of what you will come home with next." When Mom covered a tiny grin with her hand, Emma flew across the room and hugged her.

Then Brianna burst into the kitchen. "She's so beautiful. I love just watching her eat grass. What are you going to name her?"

Emma unfolded her notes. "Mrs. Holmes and I made a list of names on the way home. What do you think of Valentine? Because she is my heart horse."

"Nice."

"Or Obsidian? That's polished black volcanic glass. Super cool, huh?"

Brianna suggested. "How about Ebony or Raven? Sally is sweet."

"I love Black Magic. And Bedazzle because she is a shining jewel. Or Midnight or—"

Mom interrupted, "It's way too soon to name that horse since we don't know if it can stay."

Emma walked to the window to look at the mare. *Oh, she's staying all right, and she needs a name.* "She's the softest thing ever. Kinda like the pink pillow on your bed."

"My velvet one?" Brianna asked.

"That's it. It's the word I thought of when I first touched her." Emma dipped her chin in a decisive nod. "Her name is Velvet. Black Velvet."

After dinner that night, she cleared the table and dashed out the back door as fast as she could. The black beauty paced the far fence line.

"Easy there. This is your new home." The mare picked up speed as Emma approached. "Settle down, Velvet. Do you like your name?" She talked soothingly as she held out a piece of apple, but the horse trotted by. "Nobody is going to catch you unless you allow it—is that what you're telling me?" When Emma stepped into the horse's path, the mare spun away, shaking her head. "I hear you, but I'm not going to leave you alone. You'll love it here. I promise."

She walked fifteen feet away from the fence. "Okay. You want to run. I'm going to make you think it's my idea." As the mare passed, Emma raised her arm in the direction she was already traveling and clucked. The horse sped up, then skidded to a stop, reversed, and went past her. When the horse lowered her head, she flicked one ear toward Emma. "Thinking about being my friend yet?"

After several more turns, Emma stepped backward, and the horse stepped toward her. "That's better." Now when she offered the apple, the horse walked to within four feet of her and bobbed her head. Soon Velvet's nose inched forward, and her feet followed all the way to Emma where the horse delicately lifted the apple from her hand.

"The key to your heart is treats." Emma stroked the side of the horse's face and worked along her neck, rubbing circles and scratching. "What's this?" She fingered a strand of mane with a pink tip. When she scratched the hair with her fingernail, the pink strand broke off. She cleaned black from under her nail. "Someone dyed your mane pink and then covered it with black? You're a mystery." Her fingers combed the horse's mane.

The back door opened, and Dad stepped outside beckoning her. If Mom sent him, it'd be best to go right away. "See that window? Up there." She pointed to her bedroom. "If I'm not here, I'm there—wishing I was with you. You call me if you need me. I'll sleep with my hearing aid in and leave my window open so I can hear you. Deal?"

Emma practically danced to the house. When she got to the door, she hoped to see the mare gazing after her, but instead, the horse had run to the far end of the pasture. "You're not going to find a hole in the fence, you beautiful dreamer."

CHAPTER EIGHTEEN

SELAH

*T*hat night, Selah's Dad brought home burgers. Everyone ate in silence. Even Michael seemed to sense the tension in the room. Davy held his burger in front of his open mouth and moved his eyes from one parent to the other.

Selah nibbled on crackers. *I've lost my only lead for finding Dream. I'm going to barf.*

As they were finishing, Grandma Katie knocked and eased open the door. "Davy. Michael. Come on, little men." She bent at the waist to engage them. "Let's go play Uno with Grandpa," she whispered.

As she ushered them away, the boys walked like silent robots under her control.

"We need to be real quiet because Grandpa's still not feeling good. But he's missed you guys and is up for a couple games."

"Selah's in trouble," Davy whispered to Grandma Katie as he eyeballed the drama around his sister at the kitchen table.

Selah's laptop lay open to her social platform as her dad had instructed. Her brain frozen, she couldn't think of anything in her defense. She waited in a traumatized trance. *I thought he would help me. I had to find out what he knew—for Dream.*

Dad said, "Show me."

Selah opened messenger. "He sent me a message." She scrolled. "I don't see it."

"He's deleted the conversation then. Covering his tracks." Dad's voice was even and controlled. "That's okay. He's not going to hide from me. What's his profile name?"

"Like Red-Rover or something. But he said his name was Chip."

"Like Chip off the old block, I bet. This guy's a predator, Selah."

"Well, I didn't know." She couldn't look up. She rubbed her hands together like they were freezing. "I thought he was a teenager. There's a picture of him in front of the high school." She searched, then frowned. "It's not here."

"Do you have any idea how lucky you are?"

Nodding as Mom's icy tone pierced her, Selah focused on her hands. Her fingernails dug into her palms.

"What would have happened to you if Caroline's mom hadn't recognized the danger?" Mom's voice shrilled.

Selah didn't have any good answers. Swallowing hard, she started to speak when she caught Dad's expression and thought better of it.

"I talked to the sheriff today." Dad snapped the laptop shut, crossed his arms, and leaned on the table with his mouth tight like he was clenching his teeth. "He suggested for your own safety, you be restricted from access to *any* social media until this guy is found."

"But…" Selah sprang to her feet. "It's my best chance to find Dream."

"Sit. Down." With his eyes bulging, Dad commanded her attention. She finally understood what people meant when they said someone had steam coming out of their ears. She bit the inside of her cheek. Easygoing Dad looked like his face had fried livid red at the beach.

"You were chatting on the internet with a child predator. We try to protect you from the crazies in the world, but we need your cooperation." He tucked her laptop under his arm as he stood. "You'll be without your laptop for an indefinite time. The sheriff is having an expert go through everything to find this man."

"You're grounded, young lady." Mom got the last word. "Except for school, you may not leave the house, use a computer or a phone, or watch TV."

"Yes, ma'am," Selah said meekly. Inside, she screamed, "How will I ever find Dream?"

A moment later, Mom turned back. "I live and breathe to take care of you. I'm horrified by how close evil came to changing all of our lives." Her tearful words landed gently on Selah. "What really hurts is that you didn't come to me."

"I'm so sorry." Selah hurried to her mom and hugged her. "I should have told you about the guy. I didn't think you'd let me go, and I was desperate."

"No excuses, but I accept your apology."

Sprawled on the couch in front of a blank TV screen, Selah mindlessly flipped through a teen magazine. *Is Dream safe? Does she get enough to eat?* A high-pitched beep-beep got her attention. *Cartoons? I wasn't watching cartoons.* Davy sat cross-legged on the floor in front of her. *When had he come in the room?*

"You're home already? Have fun with Grandpa?"

Davy shot a glance at her and then faced the screen. "We only played one game, and he had to lie down. We got graham crackers and milk. Then Mom picked us up."

"Strange. Grandpa's battle cry is 'one more game'."

He changed the channel to a Roy Rogers and Trigger show.

The minute the famous palomino horse appeared on the screen, Selah broke. *I need Dream.* She leapt from the couch and ran to the barn. Sitting on a hay bale with her knees tucked to her chest, she longed to redo that awful day when Dream was taken. She would change everything. She would put a lock on Dream's stall. If only she'd branded the horse with something that would tell evil to stay away. *Grandma Mary's brand.* Selah jumped from the hay bale and dug into a storage cabinet finally pulling out the brand. Grandma Mary's Illusion was the first to wear the horseshoe with the sunlit cross, and Dream would be the next. As soon as she came home.

Then Selah searched for her dad. *He might have news of Dream.* She peeked into the bedroom. Intent on his reading material, he didn't seem to notice her intrusion. Comfortably settled into an old lounge chair, he balanced a Forest Service Training Manual on his crossed leg. She eased into the quietness and slipped onto the arm of the chair. "Training?"

He answered without looking up. "I'm teaching a class next week."

"Ah. I'm glad you like your job. Living at the farm is the best. Grandpa next door and Sweet Dream..." The horse's name caught in her throat.

Dad highlighted a sentence of text. "I understand. I grew up in this house, and I love it here."

"I'm sorry about going to The Grill. I was desperate and dumb."

"No argument for me on that. Don't let it happen again."

"Yes, sir."

"I had to call the movie producer and tell her about Dream." He inhaled deeply and blew it out fast. "She was understanding and said to tell you how sorry she is."

"It keeps getting worse. But you know what? I don't even care about the movie anymore." She crossed her arms around herself.

"Life has a way of putting things into perspective, doesn't it?"

"You mean what's important and what's not?"

He nodded.

"I thought making a movie was the most important thing ever. Boy, was I wrong. Grandpa is. Dream is. Our family is."

"Tough lessons."

"Did you talk to the police again?"

"They don't know anything." He closed the manual. "They finally located Cade Taylor, but no evidence directly links him to Dream's disappearance."

"He's a thief. She didn't just disappear. He stole her. It's been a whole week, and we still know nothing."

"They said he was cooperative and answered all the questions to their satisfaction." Dad tossed the manual onto the table, pulled her into his lap, and hugged her. "Taylor said he'd delivered horses from Louisiana to the show, and it checked out."

"Have they found any of the other stolen horses?"

"No, and they have no leads."

"Please say April Fools, Daddy." She nestled into his chest, and tears wet his cotton shirt. He held her tightly and let her anguish cry itself out. "I'm so sorry I worried you and mom. My heart feels empty. Like Dream's gone forever. Dream can't help herself—she'll be a bunch of trouble. He'll figure out quick he needs to keep her drugged to sell her as a safe riding mount." She shivered. She put one hand on Dad and pushed herself away to gauge his reaction. "I think he sold her for dog food." She waited for him to deny her worst fear, but he only stared out the window.

When the phone rang, Dad shifted her to pick it up. His eyes opened in alarm. "I'm on my way." He jumped up, sliding Selah onto her feet, and headed for the door.

His alarm frightened her. "What?"

"Your grandpa. Gotta go."

She raced behind him. "Grandpa?"

"Help your mother put the boys to bed." Grabbing his cap, he yelled, "Karen! I've got to run to Dad's. Something's wrong over there."

Mom flew to his side. "What's going on?"

"I'm not sure. Katie called, but was incoherent." Dad patted his pockets, then flipped out his keys.

"Oh dear. Go."

Selah ran on his heels, jumped into the car, and shut the door. Buckling her seat belt, she turned to him, her face resolute.

Dad shifted into gear and roared down the driveway. After speeding a quarter mile on the country road, he whipped into

Grandpa and Katie's driveway. As they neared the house, Selah's eyes fixed on the flashing lights. Dad spun off the gravel drive into the grass and stopped next to the running ambulance. A young man in a white shirt with patches on his sleeves shut the ambulance's back door and trotted to the cab. The sirens blared as they sped away. The front door stood open. Katie moved around inside and soon came running out toting her purse and a sweater. She tugged open the back car door and slid into the backseat. "Canaan Regional."

Dad spun the car and drove after the ambulance. "What happened?"

"He'd been feeling off this afternoon. Took a long nap. He picked at his food at dinner. After one game with the boys, he went to lie down. I was cleaning up after the boys' snack when I heard his book hit the floor." The tires squealed as Dad made a turn. "When I went to check on him, he was holding his chest. He couldn't talk, and he was barely breathing. I called 911 right away." Katie struggled to finish. "Thank God, they got here so fast."

A choke cut off Grandma Katie's voice, and Selah's breath caught in her throat. "Grandpa." Fear gripped her, and tears swelled in her eyes.

Nothing could ever be worse than losing Grandpa. *Nothing.* Katie sniffled in the back seat. Selah closed her eyes and begged. *Take Sweet Dream. But please... don't take my grandpa.*

CHAPTER NINETEEN

EMMA AND BLACK VELVET

The next morning, Emma rolled over stretching her arms wide and sighed with the contentment that came from great sleep. Her heart swelled with happiness. She popped up to look out the window and make sure the horse she bought yesterday was not a dream. She gasped. The pasture was empty. She pressed closer to the window and peered into every nook of the field. There was nowhere for the horse to hide. She spotted the gate—the *open* gate. "You stinker. You can open gates?" She scrambled to pull on jeans and a sweatshirt. "If you make me miss church, Mom is ..." She couldn't complete the sentence. She ran down the stairs.

Mom wore an apron over her church dress and studied Emma as she burst into the kitchen. "You're in a hurry," Mom spoke and signed.

"I have to check on Velvet." Emma rushed out the back door. After grabbing the halter, she leapt onto her bike. Her panic pedaled after the mare. *My horse is running away.* She followed the hoof-shaped divots in a beeline across the lawn. "Don't make me chase you all the way to your old house. I will if I have too." The horse's trail led directly to Mrs. Holmes's Welsh Pony farm. "Ah... sweetness, you wanted a friend."

Emma gasped when she spotted the frenzy at the farm. The herd stallion ran his mares from one end of the fifty-acre pasture to the other. Leading the herd was Emma's mare. "You're good at making trouble."

Standing by the barn with her hands cupped around her mouth, Mrs. Holmes called the herd to come in. They thundered past her and disappeared behind a stand of trees.

Emma came and stood at her side. "I'm so soooo-so sorry."

Mrs. Holmes rested her hand on Emma's shoulder and turned her toward the hay barn. "Hopefully, eating will have more appeal than galloping and losing weight." The wind tore many of the words away. "Help me get hay out."

Together, they heaved two bales of hay onto the golf cart. Emma cut the strings and tossed one section of hay at a time as Mrs. Holmes steered through the pasture. Sure enough, on the herd's next pass, a few of the mares peeled away and went for the hay. Soon the rest of the herd gave up the gallop and gathered around the hay banquet. The stallion took his kingly position on a dirt mound. Velvet stood apart from the others. Her sides heaved with exertion, but her spirit remained alert and ready to run.

"Not the best way to introduce a new horse to a herd." Mrs. Holmes chuckled. "I hope she was here for the company of the mares and not my handsome gentleman."

Emma wished she was better at reading lips or had a better hearing aid. She put pressure on the device to hold it more firmly in her ear. If only she could glue it in!

"From the way she's flipping her tail at him, she thinks he's fabulous. We need to get her out of there. I wonder how long she's been running with my herd."

As she spun to gallop along the fence, Velvet's hooves launched dirt skyward. The bay stallion thundered after her.

"She doesn't look like the horse we bought yesterday, does she?" Emma swelled with happiness and marveled at the mare's power and beauty. She felt taller, stronger, special.

"There isn't any doubt they drugged her. Looks like they've worn off now. I hope and pray she doesn't turn out to be too much for you to handle."

The doubt dried out her mouth. She hoped and prayed the same thing.

"She won't be easy to catch. I need to bring my stallion into the paddock. I'll promise him food." Mrs. Holmes threw open double gates to the paddocks outside the barn. The band of mares knew that was the dinner bell. They abandoned the hay and bunched into the paddock. Mrs. Holmes waved toward the feed buckets lining the fence and gestured emptying a cup. "Can you get grain for them?"

While Emma lured the mares with food, Mrs. Holmes shut the gate behind them and opened the stallion's area. She whooped and hollered and clanged the metal feed scoop on the gate hinge. The stallion stopped and looked her way, then resumed pursuit of his new mare.

"Oh dear. He likes her. More than food. I'll go after him." She hurried to the barn and grabbed his halter and lead rope.

They jumped on the golf cart, driving out to the horses. Velvet stood like a statue while the stallion pranced around her. His neck arched like a swan.

Mrs. Holmes leapt from the cart before it came to a complete halt. She spoke to him in a quiet commanding voice. She advanced toward him and swung a training stick to ask him to back away from her and the mare. When he obeyed, she leaned toward him with her hand out. He eyed the bribe and walked to accept her offer. As she slipped the halter over his tapered nose, she spoke kindly to him. "Handsome man. Let's walk to the barn. What do ya say?" Over her shoulder, she told Emma. "I'll be back to catch the mare if she doesn't follow us to the barn."

"I can do it."

"She's so full of adrenaline—I doubt she'll let you catch her."

"She was running in the pasture last night, but she came to me. I'll try." Emma walked strategically toward the mare's hind end.

Velvet rotated to look at her. When Emma held out a horse cookie, Velvet politely extended her nose to take the treat.

"Too easy. I'm impressed. Good job." Mrs. Holmes's thumb popped up. "Let's take her through the barn."

Emma secured the halter. "She's super smart, but how did she get in here?" She glanced around. "She didn't open a gate to get in your pasture." Her forehead wrinkled. "She jumped the fence?"

"That's the only way."

"She's a jumper!" Emma squealed. Visions of jumping shows flooded her mind. "If she can jump that high on her own, we can do an Equitation Over Fences class easy."

Velvet walked quietly alongside her. "Did you need a friend? I get that. I don't have any friends either." Deep in thought, she slowed her steps. "I was hoping *you* would be my friend. And what do you do? You run away. Exactly how is that gonna help?"

Emma led Velvet down the driveway, past the water well and past the shed. She tugged the horse's teeth away from a shrub. "Don't eat Mom's shrubs! You'll get us in so much trouble." She yanked the evidence from the mare's mouth and tossed it away. "I need to tie the gate shut. The latch is way too easy for you—you clever thing. If you jump out and I know you can..." She wagged her finger. "My parents would say you're too much trouble and send you back to the auction. You could end up in a dog food can. Is that what you want? Think about it."

After slipping in the back door, she started to kick off her shoes when she noticed Mom. She stood in the middle of the kitchen with her purse over her arm, ready to go to church. She scrutinized Emma, then looked at the toes of her black pumps. After a deep breath, she said, "Okay. You're coming as you are." Mom paused as if considering the wisdom of her decision. "There are wet wipes in the car, and you can clean the dirt off your face and arms as we go. Hit your shoes with them too."

Emma's mind flashed to the look she would get from the Sunday school class princess. She always wore a nice dress and black patent leather shoes with clip-on, tiny bows that matched her dress. Her silky brown hair would be drawn back and French braided.

Sure enough, the princess frowned when she saw Emma.

"I know I look terrible," Emma said.

"Yes, even worse than usual."

"My horse got out, and I needed to catch her."

"You have a horse? You never told me. I never knew deaf people could ride."

"I can do anything I set my mind to do—except hear."

A dirt spot smudged the princess's dress as she linked arms with Emma. They walked arm in arm to the student worship center. "You're so lucky. I've always wanted a pony. Since my parents won't even let me get a kitten, I know I'll never get one."

"I am lucky. She's wonderful and amazing and beautiful."

"How long have you had her?"

"Since yesterday. I bought her at an auction."

"Can I come over sometime to meet her? What's her name?" The princess clung to her.

Emma studied the girl's lips. Was her hearing aid lying to her? Was the princess actually being nice?

"Would you let me ride her?"

"Would be fun, but it's too cold right now." All because of Velvet, someone wanted to be her friend. "Her name is Black Velvet. She's super soft and as black as your shoes."

CHAPTER TWENTY

EMMA AND BLACK VELVET

*E*very morning, Emma sprung from her bed and lunged for the window. She anxiously searched the pasture. Her whole body sighed with relief when she spotted Velvet right where she belonged. She'd not gotten out since that first night, but it didn't stop Emma from worrying.

It rained the rest of March and the whole month of April so all she'd done was feed and admire her beautiful horse. Someday she would ride—when she was ready. *It takes time to learn to trust each other.*

May was chock-full of end-of-school-year activities and testing. But Velvet was all settled into her new surroundings, and Emma had spent as much time as she could getting to know the horse. It seemed the horse knew way more than Emma did and was training her. Last week, though she'd been brave enough to lean on the horse's back. She hadn't been able to bring herself to throw her leg over. Today she planned to change that. And now that school was finally out, she'd have all summer to ride her. "I have big plans for you today."

When she got downstairs, Mom had different ideas. "I want you to pick up and vacuum the living room. When you finish, I'll have laundry ready to be folded and put away."

"It's vacation," Emma complained, turning her palms up. "I wanted to work with Velvet."

"Not till the chores are done. My bunco group is coming tonight, and the house needs spiffing."

"Why isn't Brianna helping?"

Mom turned, and her face hardened. "She will clean the kitchen and then go to her dance class. Unless you want to do her chores." Mom waited for an answer.

No point in arguing. "Yes, ma'am." Emma withered.

When she finished her chores, she made a sandwich. Grabbing an apple, she decided to have lunch with the one who loved her. She was sure Velvet loved her. Didn't she nicker every time Emma came out the back door? Okay, Velvet nickered at anyone who came out. Still, Emma was convinced the mare was hoping it was her. She opened the door and was rewarded by the expected nicker. Her heart swelled with joy, and her smile flashed her teeth.

She sliced hunks of apple and fed them to the mare. After Velvet polished off the core, she licked Emma's hand. "That tickles." Her voice brimmed with delight.

She dug behind the shed and dragged out several old landscape timbers to use as ground jumps. She placed them at precise four-foot intervals along the fence line. Then she brushed the horse and combed out her mane and tail. "In your own way, I know you talk to me. I wish I could understand horse. I wonder if you could learn sign language?"

More pink was showing through in her mane. Who would've dyed the horse's mane pink? "Your owner must have loved you. But dump you at a sale? Who could do such an awful thing to you?" She threw herself around the mare's neck. "I'm sorry that happened to you. You're with me now, and we'll be forever friends."

She led Velvet to Dad's shed and tied her to a ring he'd installed on the side of the building. Inside, he'd cleared a small space to put a sawhorse. Across it lay the saddle she'd borrowed from Mrs. Holmes. On the wall, he'd nailed a shelf with a hook to hold the bridle. She placed and replaced the saddle pad, fitting it just right. Then, with great care, she positioned the saddle. She rocked it to settle it perfectly behind the mare's withers and tightened the girth while keeping a watchful eye on her. Velvet accepted the saddle like a pro and didn't object to the girthing. "Whew. That went better than I thought." As she maneuvered the bridle, she was surprised Velvet seemed to be trying to help get it on. "You're more amazing every day."

While waiting for the spring rains to stop, she'd watched groundwork videos on her laptop. She couldn't wait to try out what she'd learned. She didn't have a fancy training stick, so she borrowed a fiberglass plant stake from Mom's stash. It would have to do the job. Still not quite feeling brave enough to get on the mare, she decided to do groundwork with Velvet to make sure the horse was listening and obedient. She timidly waved the stick hoping she was asking Velvet to back. "It works," she squealed when the mare backed away. "You know all this already! You're so smart. I'm the one with stuff to learn."

She stepped to the horse's hindquarters and tapped the air by her hip. Velvet pivoted her hip away, catching the lip of Emma's boot under a front hoof. "Ooh, that was almost bad. Don't crush my toes." Next time she followed the horse's movement, keeping her feet out of the way. When the horse responded with several steps around her, she mentally patted herself on the back. With a smug smile, she retightened her ponytail.

In that moment of distraction, Velvet grabbed the plastic sandwich baggy. In one motion, the mare jerked it and the jean's back pocket away. When it didn't break free, the horse flipped her head, jostling Emma and finishing the job.

Her hand hit her bottom where her pocket should have been. "You stinker." She ripped the telltale evidence from the horse's mouth. "Do you have to try so hard to get us into trouble? And that was *my* lunch."

Glad she'd left the halter on under the bridle, she tied the horse to the shed. She snuck into the house and up the stairs to her room, changed her jeans, and stuffed the evidence behind a box of books in the closet.

Then she hurried back outside. After the pocket-ripping incident, she needed to show the horse she was brave and not afraid of her. The girl and the horse stood toe to toe like in an old western movie staring at each other. "I'm ready." She tried to sound confident. "Are you?"

Velvet licked her lips and backed a step.

"That's right. You need to respect my space. You know what's coming, don't you?" Emma set a bucket next to the horse. She talked to herself to steady her nerves. "Tip the nose toward you and grab some mane. Don't be nervous, or she'll know and take advantage of me. Put your foot in the stirrup." Her confidence growing, she ever so gently patted the mare's neck. "If the horse gets upset, get out and keep the nose pulled toward you." She stuffed her foot into the stirrup. "I'm so nervous. Now slip your leg over the saddle and sit lightly." She pushed off and sprung upward to balance over the saddle seat. "Did you get all that? Something tells me you didn't need to take notes. You're a pro, aren't you?"

Then Emma sat on top of the world. Sitting in the saddle was better than any ole soft velvet pillow. Better than warm chocolate pudding. Better than anything. "If the kids at school could see us now, they'd wish they were my friend."

She squeezed her calves against the barrel of the horse. She startled when the mare stepped forward with energy. "Go easy." Soon Velvet picked up a trot, and while Emma wasn't sure she'd asked for a trot, she allowed it because it felt great. She studied the movement of the horse's shoulders to figure out which diagonal to post on. Soon they were trotting around the pasture and over the ground poles. The mare never broke stride. "Too easy for you, isn't it?"

Emma wanted to canter in the worst way but imagined herself falling flat, then having to explain to Mom. Finally, her excitement overruled her fear. "Would it be okay with you if we canter? Nice and easy. No funny stuff." Feeling secure in the saddle, she tightened her calves around the horse. Velvet gave her a smooth controlled canter. Emma sang sweetly, "Joy, joy, joy." The chorus of the old carol totally expressed the state of her heart. "Joy, joy, joy."

If only they could canter till the sun disappeared, but Black Velvet wasn't a machine. She asked the horse to slow. Surprisingly, they were both breathing hard. She rocked to the rhythm of the mare as they walked the fence line and cooled down. "Whoever trained you is amazing. You are amazing. We'll be amazing together." As she leaned forward in the saddle, she threw her arms around Velvet's neck. "I love you with all my heart."

Mom marched from the house to the car and back to the house. She paused at the door to call out. "You're not thinking of jumping that horse, I hope."

"I'm only using ground poles to learn how to rate her between fences. I was hoping to raise them a tiny bit." Emma dropped the reins and held her hands apart showing eight inches.

"Your safety vest tight?"

"Yes, Mom."

"That helmet's not going to slip, is it?"

"No, Mom."

"Okay then. I'm off to the grocery in a few, so you need to finish. I don't want you riding when I'm gone."

Emma waved as her mom went back inside. "Let's see how it goes if we raise the poles," she said to the horse. "Only a little bit." After slipping from the saddle, Emma tied the mare to the shed to tuck one end of the poles on the fence. She dashed to Dad's shed and dragged out his collection of plastic coffee cans. She propped a red can under the other end of each pole. "That's not really jumping. We can work on our rhythm though. And Mom's watching so don't kick the cans and scare yourself."

Everything the horse did was perfect. Emma trotted the mare in several small circles before pointing her nose toward the poles. She balanced forward in the saddle and imagined Mrs. Holmes instructing her in two-point position. As she pressed her heels firmly into the stirrup irons, she gripped with her knees and lifted her weight off the horse's back.

"One, two, jump. One, two, jump." As soon as they reached the end of the line of poles, Emma circled Velvet back to the beginning of the line and went again. "Joy, joy, joy." And again.

"We should take the jumps going the other way too." She reversed direction. "One, two, jump. Joy, joy, joy."

Finally, she left the poles and followed the fence. She resisted the urge to ask the mare for another canter. "The problem is you're fantastic, and I never want to get off. I guess you need to eat and rest. But Mom's leaving so I have to get off."

She worked the bridle past the horse's ears and let the bit drop from Velvet's mouth. It clanked the mare's teeth, and she resolved to hold the bit steady next time. After pulling the saddle and pad from her back, she swung them onto the rack. Then she took a rag and dried Velvet's back. "I don't need any friends as long as I have you. You are my everything."

Mom called. "I'm going now. There's tuna salad in the fridge for your lunch."

"Yum." *Not letting Velvet anywhere near my food this time.*

As Mom opened the car door, she added, "And call Mrs. Holmes. She has some exciting news for you."

"News?" She turned the horse loose. Then she flew to the house and grabbed the hearing-aid-compatible phone, holding it to her ear. "Mrs. Holmes. It's Emma. Mom said to call you right away."

"You'll be excited about my news. My old friend and riding buddy, Jennifer, is leading a 4-H group this year. She needs a covered arena. She wants to bring her 4-H kids to my place for their mounted meetings."

Other kids who ride horses. Emma's mind raced.

"There are six girls, all close to your age. They finished Show Judging classes, and now they will work on jumping. I told her about you and Velvet, and she'd be happy to have you in the club. Want to join?"

Emma sucked her upper lip between her teeth and clamped down on it. She hated groups and clubs. She never fit in. But these were horse girls. "Yes!" she bleated, sounding very much like a cartoon goat.

"I told her you would. The first meeting is next Saturday."

"Do I bring Velvet?"

"Absolutely."

The next few days were busy ones. Not only was Emma spending as much time in the saddle as she could, but she also cleaned the tack and worked to remove a stain on her breeches. She held up horse T-shirts in the mirror until finally deciding on the blue with the gray horse. She didn't have a shirt with a black horse, and she needed to fix that problem.

On Saturday, she brushed Velvet until she was gorgeous, tacked her, and led her down the road to Mrs. Holmes's farm. A couple of the 4-H kids had already been dropped off, and Miss Jennifer arrived with three more. The horses stood tied to the trailers, and the kids moved around getting them ready to ride. The team dressed in matching T-shirts with a 4-H logo.

The moment Emma saw them laughing, she knew she wouldn't fit in. If she could hardly hear the funny things they said to each other, how could she fit in? She looked away and had started to turn back when one of the girls came running to her.

"Hi," she signed. "I'm Alana. Miss Jennifer said to watch for you and introduce you to the others."

"You're deaf too?"

Her black ponytail bounced as Alana shook her head. "My older sister is deaf, and she taught me to sign. I've been signing since I was born, almost. Come meet everyone." Alana gathered the group and introduced them.

One girl stood right in front of Emma and talked in big exaggerated mouth movements. She waved a club T-shirt and offered it to her.

Too bad people didn't understand better what it was like to be deaf. But the girl was trying. So Emma smiled. "If it's not too noisy, I can hear most tones in this ear." She tapped her left ear. "I have a hearing aid. It's not perfect, but it usually helps. Thanks for the shirt."

"You do talk kinda funny. But you can ride, and that's what makes us friends."

It was true. She did talk kinda funny, but she enjoyed being included. As everyone returned to getting their horses ready, she slipped into the barn to put on the club shirt. *I'm going to love 4-H. The kids look at me as a horse girl like them. Not a freaky deaf girl nobody can talk to.* Would they change their minds when her mom and sister took positions in the arena to sign instructions for her? *What would her new friends think?*

Thankfully, none of them seemed to notice or care that her mom and sister were hanging around. The jumps were way higher than the eight inches she'd jumped at home. She wasn't worried because Velvet could do that—easy. After all, she'd cleared a four-foot fence all on her own.

After the jumping class, a couple of the girls raved about Velvet. "She's a great jumper, and you're a great rider," said the girl who thought she needed to move her mouth real big to be understood.

Emma soaked it up and joined in the banter. "Velvet's a little too great sometimes. She pretends to be an antelope if she wants out of the pasture."

"She never even clipped a rail."

Another girl said, "My horse won't jump one inch higher than he has to, and he usually knocks a rail down. I've thought about changing his name to Touch Down." She laughed at her own joke and took her horse off toward the trailer.

"You should bring her to our next show," another girl encouraged.

"You think so?"

"Oh, definitely. She'll take home ribbons," Alana said before she led her horse away to untack.

Emma walked Velvet toward home. "That wasn't too bad. The girls seemed to like us." Miss Jennifer drove past, and the kids hung out her truck window waving goodbye. As Emma waved back, the welling tears caught her off guard. She felt both happy to the moon and sad that she never had friends before. "Thanks to you, I have friends, Velvet."

CHAPTER TWENTY-ONE

SELAH

hree weeks after the theft of Sweet Dream

Selah slipped into the all-too-familiar hospital elevator. Since the night the ambulance took Grandpa to the hospital, she spent as much time as possible with him. It helped that he was in a regular room now instead of intensive care and the hours she could visit weren't restricted.

As she eased inside his room, she set Grandma Katie's bag of clean clothes on the chair. The telltale weeks' worth of books stacked in the corner suggested Katie had done more reading than sleeping while she watched over him.

A rich, spicy aroma billowed from the diffuser. Thieves essential oil. Katie took no chances, there might be superbugs floating around in his room. In the darkened room, curled in the chair by his bed, Grandma Katie read a book by flashlight. She'd hardly left Grandpa's side since the night they'd almost lost him.

Katie rose and hugged her. She drew Selah into the hallway. A food server steered a cart around them before parking it a few doors down. "Glad you're here." Katie gave her another quick hug. "My animals behaving for you?"

"Pretty much, except the goats. As cute as the little ones are, I'll never have goats." With a sigh, she asked, "How's Grandpa? He doesn't look any better."

"He mostly sleeps. He's exhausted from all the tests they've run, but at least, now they finally know what the problem is. They started him last night on a different, super-antibiotic because they found the infection. It's in the sac that surrounds his heart."

Selah realized she was holding her breath. "His heart? I didn't know a heart had a sac."

"The doctor said we should see improvement within forty-eight hours if it works at all."

"It's *got* to work!" She dug her nails into her palms. "I want life to go back to the way it was. Grandpa healthy. Sweet Dream in the pasture where she belongs. She could be anywhere."

The scent of garden flowers enveloped her when Katie planted a delicate kiss on her cheek. "Be thankful for this day, even with all its problems. You never know...." Katie patted her hand. "Did your dad bring you?"

"He'll be up soon. He swung into the cafeteria to get us breakfast. Seems like the only thing he says to me anymore is 'eat'. And before you jump on me too—I can't eat. Everything makes my mouth and stomach sour."

"You can't afford to get any thinner. But okay." Katie held up her hands like stop signs. "I won't make it an issue. Thanks for bringing my clothes. I know you want time with him. So while you're here, I'll get cleaned up."

Selah hugged her for a long moment. She opened the door an inch at a time, careful not to wake Grandpa and tiptoed toward the bed. His white hair was neatly combed, but his face was almost as white as his hair. The oxygen cannula had shifted, so she repositioned it carefully. The sheets and blankets covering him were smoothed and neat like Grandma Katie had made the bed around him.

As she settled into a chair, she studied his breathing and was soon breathing in sync with him. *Nobody loves me like you do. You listen to me and care about my life—what makes me happy and what hurts.* "I love you, Grandpa. Please get well," she whispered.

Even when I'm rotten, you bring me donuts. How many afternoons have we spent at Ruth's Soda Shop? Two straws in a giant strawberry milkshake. How many banana splits have we shared? I remember sitting in your lap when I was little and you'd let me steer the truck in the pasture. It was our little secret. Selah's tears fell freely, and she didn't bother to wipe them away. The memory of his hands closed over hers on the steering wheel would always be a tender one. *I've lost Dream. I can't lose you.*

Next to the diffuser, on the ledge over a room air-conditioner, rested his Sunday hat. She lifted it and fingered the blue feather in the hatband. She'd been so happy when she found it in the pasture and presented it to him with the glee of a five-year-old. She thought it was a treasure. Grandpa must have too since he kept it on his hat. Over the years, he'd taught her more about blue jays than she wanted to know. She smiled recalling his science lecture on blue jay feathers. He'd explained they aren't really blue, but rather the light we see is blue, reflected from the teeny barbs on the feather. She shook her head, but she treasured the memory. "Oh, Grandpa." Leaning forward, she rested her crossed arms on the bed and lay her head down. A few minutes later, she felt his hand stroke her hair.

"Hey, sunshine. You wipe those tears away. I'm gonna be fine. The Good Lord is far from done with me."

At the strength in his voice, her heart rejoiced. "You're better. I've been so scared." While she smiled at him, tears flowed down her cheeks like rain off the brim of Grandpa's hat. "I've been praying and praying for you."

"I'm grateful. And I appreciate how much you've helped Katie." He gently rubbed her hand with his thumb. "Any news on Sweet Dream?"

As her throat tightened, she couldn't speak. She answered with a quick shake of her head. She breathed relief when Dad showed up bearing food, causing a distraction.

"Looks like you've turned a corner and are roaring back." Dad slipped an arm around Selah and hugged her. "We've all been mighty worried. Especially this one." While he grinned at Grandpa, he commanded her to eat and handed her a breakfast egg wrap.

"I was just telling Selah, I still have a lot of life lessons to share with her and the boys."

She smiled for him, even as her spirit grieved her lost horse. *After the stunt I pulled going to meet that strange man, I'm grounded from social media—probably for life. And my Sweet Dream is forever—gone. But Grandpa is better.* Real warmth crept into her smile.

"Eat."

Dutifully unwrapping the taco, she took a bite. *Life goes on even with a busted heart.*

Another three weeks later...

Selah slid a batch of oatmeal cookies from the oven as Dad came into the kitchen.

"Smells wonderful. I like that you're learning to bake." He peered over her shoulder and snatched a warm cookie.

"They're for Grandpa. He's hardly eating. He can't resist oatmeal cookies with chocolate chips. Then Katie wants me to play checkers with him long enough for her to get her hair cut. She says, if we don't keep an eye on him, he'll be out trying to mow the pasture."

"Can't keep a good man down. Has Cooper heard anything new about Dream?"

"Talked to Jordan yesterday. Dream's just disappeared into thin air."

"What about the other two horses?" Dad asked.

"No sign of them either. Jordan won't say, but I can tell she thinks they all made a quick trip to the slaughterhouse." Selah stared into the pasture where her horse should've been. Her face sagged. If she didn't change the subject fast, she'd embarrass herself by bawling—again. "You're home early?"

"I'll be over as soon as I change. Katie asked me to check the water well." Dad nibbled on the cookie. "Is it time you thought about getting another horse? Maybe talk to Laura? She still has my mom's horse and as far as I know a couple of her fillies. I bet she would give you another horse. Your grandma Mary would want that. It was so important to her that you have a descendant of her horse."

Selah didn't mean to, but she slapped the cookie spatula on the counter. "I can't just get a new Sweet Dream. She was one in a million." She blinked her tears away. No point in crying. "And no, I can't think about another horse. Not now or ever. I'll never give up looking for Dream." She wrapped foil around a plate mounded with cookies. "Going to Grandpa's." Anguish rushed out the door with her and clung to her all summer.

Restricted from all internet usage, Selah tried to find Dream the old-fashioned way. She spent hours at the library going through a reference book of horse businesses. She cross-referenced them with the lists Caroline printed of vet offices, stables, horse farms, feed stores, anywhere she might try. After a phone call, Selah would put a flyer in the mail with a personal note asking them to post it and call her if they learned anything about Sweet Dream.

Every time Dad got gas, he picked up the local sales flyers, and she called the seller of any horse even close to Dream's description.

She called each of her and Dream's sponsors, and while they were understanding, they weren't in the business of lost horses. They nicely declined to use their massive internet presence to help.

Someday, somehow, all this will pay off, and someone will see you and know you belong to me. I'll never give up. I know you're out there somewhere. Someday—I will find you.

CHAPTER TWENTY-TWO

EMMA AND BLACK VELVET

*A*s the summer passed, Emma spent every moment possible with Velvet. She felt like she'd grown to be one with her horse. She never missed a 4-H meeting with her friends, and every week, she became a better rider. School would start way too soon, despite her prayers for an endless summer.

As Emma arrived at Mrs. Holmes's, the vet latched the metal box in the truck bed and drove away. "Anything wrong?"

"All good here. I have the vet check my older mares a couple times during the year to make sure they're not having any problems with the pregnancy. Helps me sleep at night. He'll come again in January before the mares start foaling."

"A field full of foals is even better than one full of flowers." Emma pinched an imaginary flower in her fingers moving it from one side of her nose to the other as if she could smell it.

"And just like flowers, they are gone way too soon. It's hard to love them so much and have to let them go to their forever homes," Mrs. Holmes's expression wilted momentarily. "Say, the club is going in a few weeks to a Schooling show at Fox Glen. Want to go?"

"I don't know... that costs money?"

"The entry fees are reasonable. Jennifer asked if I would pick up two of the girls who live nearby, and I could take you along too. You're ready. You and Velvet are a terrific team, and if you don't come home with the High Point Champion award—well, I'll be shocked."

"Wow. You really think we're that good? I'd love to do a show, but I have to ask Mom."

"Yes, you are that good, and I asked your mom before I asked you." Mrs. Holmes tossed her hands up to frame her big smile. "She took a couple of days to think it over. Then she said yes."

"My mother? Said yes?" Emma's initial excitement choked off with a horrifying thought. *I can't.* "I'd be so embarrassed with Mom and Brianna in the show ring signing to me. I'd rather not go."

"I didn't get the impression she plans to do that. You'll need to ask her. I'm sure the show will accommodate any special needs."

"No way. Can't happen. I would just die." One palm up and one palm down, Emma rolled her hands over emphasizing her death.

After bursting into the back door, she searched the house for Mom, finding her at the sewing machine. When Mom looked up, Emma blurted, "You wouldn't stand in the ring at the show to sign the instructions. Would you?" she spoke and signed with urgency. "I would be so embarrassed. I can follow along with what the other kids do. Please let me be one of the normal kids."

Mom turned off the machine's light, leaned back in the chair, and opened her arms. "You're a completely normal girl. You have all of the important things right."

Emma flew into her hug.

"You are thoughtful, caring, helpful, and considerate. The things of your heart are what count." Mom kept her hug tight. "But to put your mind at rest, I'm not going to sign the instructions. You don't need me there."

Heat flushed her cheeks. It pleased Emma that her mom saw so much good in her. But then, suddenly self-conscious, she let her smile waver as she turned inward where she usually hid.

During the next weeks, Emma begged Mrs. Holmes for extra riding lessons, practiced at home, and cleaned her tack. The day before the show, Emma spent the entire afternoon getting ready. With an extra small and extra soft face brush, she stroked Velvet. The mare closed her eyes. "Aww... you love that. Sweet girl. I bet someone used to do that for you. It was mean—your owner sent you away to an auction. It's you and me now. Forever and ever."

When Emma finished, Velvet's mane and tail didn't have a single knot. She wished more of the old pink highlights would show. "You're perfect in pink. We should fix that." She kissed the horse's nose and went in search of pink.

She found Mom on the couch and snuggled beside her.

Mom scrunched her nose. "Been with the horse?"

Emma smiled, her heart content as if she lounged by a campfire with hot chocolate.

"Want a new book?"

"About horses?"

Mom angled her head to look her in the eyes. "How long have I been your mother? Of course, it's a horse book. I've always encouraged you to read—I just never expected reading horse books could translate to owning a horse." She lifted it off the shelf and displayed *Ride Your Dream Horse*. "Reading mysteries didn't inspire you to be a detective."

"But horses are magical. I've wanted one since you first took me to Mrs. Holmes to show me the new foals." Emma beamed, snatching the book to her chest. "Thank you. I love it."

"So that's where I went wrong."

She flashed a toothy smile. "I'll save it for later. I'm trying to get ready for the show. First thing is a new battery for my hearing aid so I can hear the instructions in the ring."

"In the junk drawer in the kitchen."

"Do we have any pink crepe paper?"

"Whatever for?"

"In the craft book you got me for Christmas is an article explaining soaking crepe paper in hot water and then using it to dye hair."

"No." Mom's serene expression contorted. "Pink hair will not make you more beautiful. You're beautiful because you have a kind and generous—"

"Heart." Emma finished the sentence drawing a heart in the air. "I know, Mom. You tell me all the time. It's not for my hair—it's for Velvet's mane. It would look cute if I put a little matching pink right here." She separated and wagged a clump of hair. "Velvet had pink highlights when we got her. She'll be gorgeous."

"Her mane is black."

"Somebody covered the pink with black something. When I saw a tiny patch peeking out, I scraped more black off, but I broke the strand. I decided to let it wear off on its own except it's been months now."

"How strange. Why would anybody do that?"

"I can't figure it out. Unless the owner thought she wouldn't sell with a pink mane."

"We have crepe paper left over from Brianna's birthday party. Look in the upstairs hall closet."

By the time Emma finished with styling Velvet's mane, it was nearly dark. "Sleep standing up, would you? For me?" As if on cue, Black Velvet dropped to her knees, flopped on her side, and rolled. Emma closed her eyes. "Aargh."

So nervous about the show, Emma hardly slept. Velvet hadn't escaped the pasture since her first night, but that didn't keep Emma from worrying. First thing in the morning, she sprang to the window and searched the pasture. When she found her horse, a sigh of relief forced the tension from her body. "This would have been the worst day for you to escape." She needed to be ready to load Velvet into Mrs. Holmes's trailer to leave for the horse show by seven thirty a.m. "Trailer! I forgot about the trailer. Please let Velvet walk right in."

Before Emma could tack her up, Velvet needed another good brushing. "You had to roll didn't you?" The process felt natural. But even though her confidence grew, the trailer-loading issue nagged her. She tucked a boot rag into her waistband and hung the bridle on her shoulder. "Let's go, beautiful. It's our day to shine."

When she got to Mrs. Holmes's farm, the trailer was hooked to the truck, and the door to the trailer stood open. As they neared the horse compartment, Velvet's head raised, and the whites of her eyes showed. The mare relaxed when Emma led her past the trailer and tied her at the barn. She made her way down the aisle of the barn to Mrs. Holmes's office. The light was on so she cracked open the door. "I'm here."

Mrs. Holmes laid aside her papers. "Yeah. Let's get going then. It's a big day. Is Velvet ready?"

"I sure hope so. I thought it was a good omen she was even in the pasture. But when we walked by the trailer, I noticed her head go up, and she looked at it with wide eyes. I should have practiced loading her this week."

"Oh goodness, you're right." Mrs. Holmes plopped both hands on the side of her face. "It's been so busy around here, it never crossed my mind. We can only hope the reason she was so bad getting into the trailer at the sale barn was because she might be one of those horses that has a bad reaction to being drugged." Mrs. Holmes turned out the light and ushered Emma from the office. "Oh dear, oh dear, let's go see what we have to deal with."

Velvet stood tied right where Emma had left her. "She seems quiet enough." She crossed her fingers as she approached Velvet. "I'm sure she'll get right in—for me. She'll do anything for me."

"Let's take her saddle off first and then entice her with food so she gets in on a good note." Mrs. Holmes slipped into the feed room and dipped out molasses-soaked crimped oats. "This will call to her, and she will follow you anywhere." Mrs. Holmes stepped into the horse trailer and sprinkled a bit of feed into the manger. Then she rattled feed in the scoop.

Velvet's ears perked, and she licked her lips. The horse stepped toward the trailer, sniffing the feed and pulling Emma along. The horse leaned into the horse trailer but balked at putting a foot on the ramp.

"Ask her to step in, and I'll jiggle the food."

The horse backed away as if a bee stung her on the chest.

Emma's mind flashed to the night at the auction when it took six men to load the horse in the trailer. She didn't have six men today. "Velvet, please get in. You can trust me. I wouldn't ask you to do anything that might hurt you. Please, Velvet. We'll have so much fun." She wiggled the rope. She pulled the rope. She tugged the rope. She snapped the rope.

Velvet took a definite step backward.

"Do her groundwork exercises. Get her feet moving as fast as you can. Then let her stand quietly by the door."

Emma got to work. She put hustle into the horse's feet and wouldn't let her stop until she was looking into the trailer. The horse seemed to get more agitated and uncooperative by the moment. The mare's whole body trembled when she belted out a whinny. Mrs. Holmes's herd stallion answered the distress call and galloped in from the field.

"She's getting worse."

"I'm so sorry, Emma. I could get a butt-rope and a lunge whip, but I think she'd fight. That would put her in the wrong frame of mind to do her best in a show."

Emma slumped, and she bit her lip to keep it from pouting. "I don't want to scare her or lose the trust she has in me. She has a good reason she won't load. She didn't want anything to do with the trailer at the auction. Then those bullies came and stuffed her in."

"Will take a lot of patience and kindness to overcome that. I'm sorry, but I've got to go now. The other girls are waiting on me to pick them up. I feel terrible. We'll figure this mystery out with her and take her to the next show." Mrs. Holmes latched the trailer door and hugged Emma. "Take her home and ask one of your parents to drive you to the show. You can learn a lot by watching the others and ground support is always needed. You know where it is. Hope to see you there."

Emma blinked back tears as she resaddled her horse. *This was going to be the best day of our whole life.* When Velvet nudged her, she slipped a hand under her mane. "It's not your fault," she whispered.

As Mrs. Holmes drove away, Emma sank onto a bench outside the barn. She stared in a daze across the pasture. The stallion stood by the fence for another few minutes before tossing his head, throwing his mane from side to side, and galloping back to his herd.

"We were going to win a ribbon today." She sulked as she fiddled with the lead rope in her hand. "I can't ride you on the road. It takes a long time to get there in a car. I'm not mad at you. You can't help it." She pushed herself up off the bench. "Something about the trailer scares you—I get that. I should've worked on loading. Let's go home." Shoulders slumped, she trudged down the driveway, leading Velvet. When she got to the farm's front gate, her gaze lifted off into the distance. "Everybody will be there. Except us," she sighed. Then she spotted the opening in the trees. "Wait. Fox Glen is that way. It can't be too far." She'd ridden in the woods with Mrs. Holmes. They'd never gone as far as Fox Glen but… "I'll bet I can find it." She slipped on the bridle and tightened the girth. Emma moved Velvet next to the fence, climbed to the top, and wiggled into the saddle. She turned the mare's nose toward the trees and urged her into a trot.

The trail through the woods was wide and sandy. Velvet acted like she'd ridden the trail every day of her life. Her trot was eager and confident. Emma posted to the rhythm of the ground-covering trot.

When a large red-tailed hawk flew across the trail, Velvet slammed on her brakes. Her whole body tensed. Emma felt the horse shift her weight to her hindquarters as if she was planning to pivot and escape.

"Easy, beautiful. Hawks eat mice, not horses." As Velvet stood frozen and tense, Emma reconsidered her plan to ride to the show. She set her hands wide and low to the saddle, bracing should the horse spook. "If you drop me and run home, I'm afraid of what Mom would do, and you should be too." She sat quiet in the saddle while her heart slowed. When Emma puffed a frustrated breath, Velvet flicked an ear toward her. "You would've been beautiful with a blue ribbon hooked to your bridle."

Even if they did get to the show, what would her parents say when they found out she rode through the woods by herself? "We have to go back." With the horse still on high alert, she backed Velvet away from the spot where they encountered the hawk. When the mare quieted, she turned the horse around and headed home. "We can't win if we can't go. What is it with you and horse trailers? Why don't you trust me?"

CHAPTER TWENTY-THREE

EMMA AND BLACK VELVET

As they neared the house, Dad popped out of the garage dressed in his running shoes and shorts. He waved at her. "Thought you were going to the show with Mrs. Holmes?"

"Velvet was afraid to get in the trailer," Emma pouted. Then a brilliant idea, a gift from heaven, flipped her frown into glee. "Dad! The show is at Fox Glen. Mrs. Holmes told me once, it's only three miles if you cut through the woods." She lay the reins down and signed. "Would you run with us? Then I could ride to the show."

He dipped into a knee squat and stretched. "Sure. Why not? I'll tell your mom. We were going to drive over in a bit to watch you ride. I can run there instead. Be right back."

"Yes!" She tensed as she waited. Velvet tipped her head to look at her with one eye. "You'll see—we're going. You'll be bringing home a ribbon today."

Dad stuck his head in the house and called for Mom. Emma couldn't hear what he told her, but Mom stood in the doorway with her arms crossed. From the look on her face, this plan was over before they'd gotten going. But, though Mom didn't smile, she didn't object either. Then Dad started jogging in place, and they were good to go.

"How should this work? Should you go first or what?"

"We'll follow you."

"Alrighty then. We're off." Dad jogged toward the path.

As she trotted behind her dad on the forest trail, her mind raced ahead to arriving at the show. Mrs. Holmes and the 4-H team would be so surprised. Her giggle transformed her face with a smile. Picking up on Emma's energy, the horse surged forward and leapt into a canter. Emma settled the mare back to a trot. "Steady there. I didn't ask you to canter. Save your energy for the show." From two-point position, she whispered to the mare, "And don't run over Dad."

A couple of small white-tailed deer bounded away. The mare flicked one ear in their direction but otherwise didn't seem to care. "Hawks are dangerous, but not deer. Check."

Velvet tensed and snapped her attention toward a thicket. Emma gripped the reins. The tips of her nails dug into her palms. Twenty feet ahead, Dad stopped abruptly. Velvet followed his cue and halted. Dad pointed to his eye and then toward the bushes to the right of the trail. Emma sucked in a breath. A muscular, longhaired dog crossed the path way too close. Its head rose high. Once it started barking, it hopped stiff-legged on its front feet, bounding toward them. A dark-brown mangy dog sprang onto the path beside the yellow cur.

Dad stepped off the trail and grabbed a fallen limb. The dogs rushed forward snapping at him. Stepping back, he swung his stick and missed. As he tripped on a root, he fell to the ground. The yellow dog lunged at him.

Velvet clamped the bit in her teeth, yanking Emma forward in the saddle. Emma shrieked as she clung to the horse's neck. When the mutt's teeth flashed at Dad, the mare's hoof struck the dog's leg. It yelped and skittered sideways trying to escape. The second, taller dog raced in and nipped at Velvet's hind leg. As quick as a flash of lightning, just before the dog's teeth snapped on her leg, the mare nailed the dog with a hoof to his rib cage. The breath knocked out of it, the dog dropped to the dirt and whimpered as it crawled off the path.

Emma adjusted her seat in the saddle and slipped her feet back in the stirrups. "Are you okay, Dad?"

"I think so." His face red and angry, he massaged his hip as he climbed to his feet. He stood beside the horse and rested his hand on her neck. After giving the mare a thank-you pat, he signed, "Are you all right?"

"I'm okay. Velvet is amazing. I feel bad for the dogs. What are they doing out here?"

"People dump their dogs along country roads. Dogs gone wild are more dangerous than wild animals because they have no fear of people."

"Those two learned to have a healthy fear of black horses." She patted Velvet.

"I'm real glad to have her on my side. Far as I'm concerned, she's a keeper, and I'm happy to buy her hay."

"She's the best thing ever." A soft warmth filled Emma's heart as if clouds uncovered the sun. "Can you still run? We can walk."

"I'm good." Dad turned and started at a slow jog. "Let's get to the show and see what other surprises this horse has for us."

A shrill whinny alerted Emma they were close. "We found it." When they cleared the trees, they walked around the outskirts of the farm pastures.

"Go find your group. I need to cool down."

Weaving through the small crowd of people and horses, she searched for Mrs. Holmes and the girls in her 4-H club. She made her way to the trailer parking. When she slid from Velvet's back, she tied the horse to a pipe corral. She placed her hand on the mare's neck, and Velvet tipped her nose toward her. "You—are—amazing. I love you. Thanks for taking care of me and Dad." Closing her eyes and resting her forehead on the mare's forehead, she whispered, "Since I can't sign in horse *yet*, I hope you know how much I love you."

The old white station wagon bounced across the grass and parked. Her sister jumped from the car and ran toward her waving. Mom was dressed for a church picnic. She held onto her sunhat with one hand and brushed her capris with the other. "We didn't miss your class, did we?"

At least Mom was wearing sneakers. They weren't Ariat riding boots like the other mothers, but at least they weren't her usual stylish sandals.

"We just got here. We were attacked by wild dogs, and Velvet saved Dad."

"What! In our woods?" Alarm raised her voice. "I was afraid riding here was a bad idea. That's scary."

"It was scary. If those dogs ever see a black horse again, they'll be running away."

Mom angled her back to the sun and regained her composure. "You're both okay? Who knew a horse would do that?"

"We're okay because Velvet's amazing." Emma beamed. "I've got to find Mrs. Holmes. She doesn't know I'm here yet." She dashed and found the group sitting on their horses and lining the rail of a warm-up arena. After another trainer finished with her students, the arena cleared for Emma's group. When Mrs. Holmes saw Emma, she hugged her. "Glad your parents brought you. Miss Jennifer is starting the warm-up. Stand here with me, and we'll probably both learn something new."

"Velvet is here too."

"She is?"

"Dad jogged through the woods with us."

"Brilliant. Good for you. I'm so proud of you. Mount up and get in there."

While her heart skipped with joy, Emma raced to get Velvet. Mrs. Holmes opened the arena gate. The group was trotting on the rail, and Emma merged into the line. Posting in sync with the horse felt terrific. She tingled with pride at her flashy black mare with her hot-pink mane.

After the warm-up, the team gathered around Emma and Velvet. "Love her mane."

"How did you do that?"

"She's so pretty. I want to do that to my horse."

Emma swelled at being the center of attention. "Thanks. It's easy. I can show you." She lifted and finger-combed the mare's mane.

Miss Jennifer's clapping got their attention. "Anyone riding in Equitation Over Fences should be in the holding area of the main arena."

Alana pointed to herself, Emma, and then the arena. Emma's eyebrows arched, lifting her entire expression as she turned Velvet to walk beside her. Once in the holding area, she realized she was waiting to ride in her first-ever show on her first-ever own horse. Plus, she was doing it without Mom and Brianna. Beads of sweat broke out on her forehead, and her body felt like she was standing too close to a fire. She wiped the sweat from her face.

Alana let the reins slip through her fingers and signed, "First-show nerves?"

Emma bit on her lip. "I think I have hives." She scratched her shoulders and arms vigorously.

"Once you get in the ring, you can focus on your horse, and you'll be great. You'll win this class."

"Me? You think so?"

"Oh yeah. Velvet is so smooth and responsive. You can sit there and look pretty. I'm always bumping with my outside leg to keep my horse going. His real name is Slugger, but I call him Slug. He's a dear, but still a slug."

"Now I'm even more nervous."

"Ha. You're welcome."

The announcer called the class, and the gate opened. Emma filed in behind Alana, and they walked smartly along the rail. She grinned as she noticed Alana's heel tapping her gelding's flank. As her focus changed to the rhythm of the walk, Emma mentally checked her position. *The judges are always watching.* Centered and balanced in the saddle, she stretched her calves to let her heels drop in the stirrups.

Over the loudspeaker, she thought the announcer said, "Trot. Show in the posting trot, please." She watched the other riders to make sure she'd heard correctly.

Was she on the right diagonal? She concentrated on the mare's footfalls. *Feels right. We nailed it.* She sat tall and smiled for the judges.

"Reverse and trot. Reverse and trot, please."

Velvet trotted a nice round half circle, and Emma changed posting diagonals at the exact moment they straightened out on the rail. *Nailed it.* As she trotted by the stands, she caught a glimpse of Mom's smile. *Still have the canter to go.*

Another rider, on a chestnut with four white stockings moved to the inside to pass Velvet. *They look amazing.* Emma grimaced and double-checked her riding position.

She couldn't quite hear the next set of instructions. But when everyone else cantered, she figured it out. Already a beat late, she messed up her canter cues, causing Velvet to depart on the wrong lead. Quickly drawing the horse back into a trot, Emma asked again for the canter. *Whew.* The chestnut horse blocked the judges' view. *Hope they didn't see us.*

The audience reacted with a collective gasp. *My goof wasn't that bad.* Then out of the corner of her eye, she saw Alana. Slug crashed through the other horses running like a cougar clawed his back. Two horses jumped from his path. One girl flew off into the dirt. Her loose horse stampeded after Slug, its reins fluttered like flags in a stiff breeze. Alana lost her reins when the saddle slipped to one side. She clung to the mane.

"Halt your horses. Halt your horses."

Mom stood in the stands. Her mouth stretched wide open in horrified panic. Dad put one arm around her and clamped her to his side.

Miss Jennifer vaulted over the arena fencing and called to Slug. "Whoa."

Emma halted beside another rider while keeping close rein contact with Velvet. Velvet's heart pounded through the leather saddle, and Emma feared the horse might forget she was on her back. The whites of Slug's eyes blazed as he neared them. *He's so terrified.* As the gelding galloped past her, she grabbed helplessly for the bridle. When she missed catching him as he flashed by, she pointed Velvet after him and threw her energy in "yaw".

In that second, her legs flew wide and slammed on Velvet's sides. The mare bolted forward and charged along the arena rail. In a dozen strides, they came alongside Slug and Alana. Her arm outstretched reaching for the bridle, Emma pressed her leg against Velvet asking her to crowd Slug into the rail. As Slug slowed to a canter, Emma snatched his bridle and dragged his head toward her.

Together, they eased to a trot and finally a walk. Alana dropped from the saddle and fell into the dirt. Emma reached across Slug and tugged his saddle to the middle of his back. With his tack repositioned, Slug calmed. The horse stood with his feet splayed and panted from exertion and fear.

A ring steward hurried to Alana and helped her to her feet. He took Slug's reins. "Wow. That was some riding."

"Velvet seemed to know what to do."

Emma knew it was coming, but the announcement still stung. They called out her number loud and clear. "Riders Number 17, 15, and 3 are excused from the class. Please exit the arena."

Her parents met her at the exit gate. Mom gripped Dad's arm so tight her knuckles turned white. When Emma slid from the saddle, Mom snatched her into a hug. Mom's body shook as she cried.

"I'm okay." A flush sprang to her cheeks.

Mom held her away by both arms. "You're better than okay. I was petrified but so proud at the same time."

As if on cue, Velvet pressed her nose to Dad's neck and licked him. He recoiled but smiled. "That horse is one surprise after another." He kissed the top of Emma's head. "That was amazing."

As they walked to the trailer parking, the team gathered around them. Emma tied Velvet, and Alana hurried to her. Dirt and tears streaked her tan face. "I can't believe what you did. I knew I was gonna be trampled. I've never been so scared. I'm sorry you got excused from the class because of us."

"I just reacted. If I'd stopped to think about it—I would've frozen. I'm glad you're all right. It makes getting excused worth it."

"Just as we started to canter, I got stung by a bee. Poor Slugger must have gotten stung too. When he jumped, the saddle slipped. When the horse near us spooked, he must have thought he was about to die. I kinda did too." She grabbed Emma's arm as her voice faltered.

"Mom wants to take me home. I told her I wanted to stay and cheer for you. Win the Speed event for the team, okay?" Alana patted Velvet. "Thank you. You're the greatest."

After lunch, Emma fed the rest of her Fig Newtons to Velvet. Miss Jennifer stood with the team clustered around her. "In this event, you don't need to be beautiful. You need to go clean. No refusals and no knocked-down rails. Got it?" She pointed to each team member in turn. "Then your course time will decide the winner. We walked the course together so you know what to do. As you wait your turn, go over the course in your mind. Any questions?" The kids looked at each other and her. "Emma, did you get all that?" When Emma nodded and there were no questions, Miss Jennifer said, "Be safe out there, have a blast, and good luck."

By the time, Emma's turn came, she wished she could ride home instead. *But this is what we came for.* She pictured the girl with the flying braids in the video she'd watched hundreds of times. *Now it's my turn.* Emma smoothed her braids and fingered her pink ribbons. *For luck.*

The ring steward closed the gate behind her. She asked Velvet to pick up a canter, and they made a controlled quiet circle. When the buzzer sounded, she circled the horse to the first jump and urged her forward. She tensed, holding the mare too tight. One stride from the fence, the horse swung sharply away. Emma lost her balance and barely clung to the saddle. *My fault. Sorry, girl.* Regaining her seat, she guided the mare back to the jump.

With a run-out on the first jump, no way could she win. Still, this was the most fun she'd ever had. This time Velvet grabbed the bit and rocketed over the jump. Emma gripped the saddle with her knees. Her hands followed the rhythm of Velvet's canter. They leapt an oxer, a picket fence, and the orange flower boxes. She saw the other 4-H girls' fists pumping and cheering her on. She silently yelled "Yee-ha!" as they charged the last upright jump and soared. *Not bad for a deaf girl. We showed 'em.* Emma patted Velvet's neck just like the girl in the video.

A week later, Emma marched Velvet down the road to Mrs. Holmes's on a mission. "If we're going to horse shows, you need to load into the trailer. We can take all day if you want."

Emma had watched every horse trailer loading video she found on the internet. She had a plan. Thing was, she still didn't understand the problem. Velvet did everything else she'd been asked to do. "This is the battle of Jericho! I am going to walk you around the trailer until the walls fall down."

But at the sight of the open trailer, Velvet balked and backed up. "Okay, backing is good. Back. Back." Thirty minutes later,

Emma and Velvet were even farther away from the trailer. The mare showed no sign of changing her mind.

"Let's ignore the trailer." Emma pointed in the direction she wanted Velvet to travel and clucked for a trot. After five or six times around, Emma asked her to change directions. Finally, she let the mare stop and rest at the closest point to the trailer. As soon as the horse showed a sign of relaxing, Emma took one step closer to the trailer to repeat the trot circles. Velvet nearly jerked Emma off her feet as the horse scrambled away.

With a sigh, Emma walked Velvet home. "I don't want you to think I'm giving up. I never give up."

CHAPTER TWENTY-FOUR

SELAH

When school started up in the fall, Selah's internet privileges were cautiously, selectively restored. She went through the motions of school, feeling like a hollow shell. All her grades dropped a letter, but she didn't care. She used every spare moment cruising the horse sale sites and virtual community, horse bulletin boards. Every chance she got, she posted her flyer and left posts asking people if they'd seen her horse. Her pleas to her blog followers went unanswered. The trail was cold—freezing cold.

As hard as her friends, Caroline and Amanda, had tried, seven long months of searching for Sweet Dream had turned up nothing. Jordan and Mr. Cooper did all they could, but it was fruitless. Every horse she saw, she double-checked in case it might be Dream.

It would be a long time, maybe forever, before she could think about another horse. Dream was part of her, and letting her go—how could she do that? She didn't even get to say goodbye. Maybe she should grow up. Was a horse a childish idea? A fairy tale for children?

The Thanksgiving holiday was the biggest celebration her family had ever had. It had taken Grandpa all summer to get back on his feet and another couple months till he was his old self. He was again printing out pages of tourist information for a trip to Israel. Selah ate pumpkin pie for breakfast and dessert.

Glancing out the window, she spotted Buddy by the pasture gate. As he slept, his big head drooped to his knees. "You miss her too." She pulled on a jacket and went to talk to him.

His head came up, but his eyes looked dull.

"Poor old guy. I kept hoping I'd find her, but we have to face facts. She might never come home, Buddy." Pain choked off her words. "We need to get used to the idea. I should move you to Grandpa's. It's not fair to keep you here by yourself when I can see how lonely you are. At least you would have goats and sheep for company."

She scratched his withers, and the old gelding tilted his head in enjoyment. "Would you like to go for a ride?" She dashed to grab her helmet and a bridle. They strolled around the pasture for ten minutes. An empty pasture would be tough for her, but she needed to take care of Buddy. She side-passed him to the pasture gate and swung it wide open. Buddy's spirit seemed to lift as they walked the path next to the driveway. "Enjoying the change of scenery?"

As they approached Grandpa and Grandma Katie's farm, Skunk barked. "It's me, silly." As soon as she spoke to the black Aussie dog, her frenzy increased. "Ah, sweet girl, you miss going riding with us." Sliding from Buddy's back, she petted Skunk as Grandma Katie came out on the porch drying her hands on a kitchen towel.

"Buddy is lonely. I thought I'd put him in with your sheep. He already knows them."

"Good idea. He's always welcome here. After you put him up, come on in and visit with your grandpa for a bit. He'd love that."

"Me too. Be right there." As Selah walked Buddy to the pasture, she assured him, "This will be better for you. Don't think I've given up on finding your friend. I never will."

She hung the bridle with his halter and lead rope on a hook and went empty-handed to the farmhouse.

Grandpa's lounge chair was kicked back, and the TV blared. "Hey, Selah. Look. This footage is at an equestrian center in California. High winds caused electrical lines to touch or cross or something sparking a forest fire. They'd gotten about forty-five horses out of the barn, but it's not clear how many might still be in there. The barn staff had to leave them and evacuate. What an awful deal."

She stared horror-stricken. The group of terrified animals bolted from one side of the fence enclosing the center to another. A bay Arabian screeched to a stop, then pivoted in a full circle before standing tall and snorting. Flames completely engulfed the barn and the forest on three sides of the enclosure.

The footage shut off as the person jumped into a car and shouted. "Go!"

"Behind the bay!" She snatched the remote and rewound the news clip. Then she hit record and replay. "I need to see that again. There was a black horse." Her heart pounded. When the bay came into view again, she stared intently and advanced the replay frame by frame until the black horse appeared in the background. Disappointment crushed her heart. "It's not Dream. That horse has white markings on its face." As she was about to turn it off, another horse caught her eye.

"Look there, Grandpa. See the horse behind the black one? I think the markings match the pony that was stolen at the same time as Dream. The one belonging to the little girl on the next aisle over."

She grabbed the phone and called home. "Michael! Why are you answering the phone? Where's Mom?"

"She's chopping onions. She said I could answer."

"Michael, I need a hedgehog hero."

"That's me."

"Run upstairs to my room. Get the picture that's not Sweet Dream off my bulletin board. Run as fast as you can and bring it to Grandpa's."

Michael didn't answer and didn't hang up, but his feet pounded up the stairs.

While she waited, she replayed the news segment over and over. *The horse is the right size. It might be him.* After all this time, had she stumbled on a lead? If the pony in the video was Batman, maybe....

Soon Michael burst into the farmhouse door. He thrust the picture at her while flashing a toothy smile. His stuffed hedgehog rode tucked into the front of his shirt with its face right under Michael's chin.

"You are too adorable." Katie laughed.

Selah hugged him. "You're an amazing hedgehog hero. Thank you." She studied the blaze on the pony's face. Her gaze traveled back and forth between the picture she held and the TV screen. She'd stared at the picture for nine long months, but it was important to get this right.

"Grandpa?" She showed him the picture. "I think it's Batman."

"Face markings are the same. Both sorrel, but the color's hard to match exactly because of the smoke. Ears are the same shape."

"The photo shows a little white on his rear pastern on the near side. The horses are kicking up so much dust, it's hard to see." She shoved a footstool in front of the TV, climbed up, and stuck her face inches from the screen. "It's there! I knew it! That's Batman." She jumped from the stool and hugged everybody. "I have to call Mr. Cooper and the police and the ranger."

"You can call Cooper—he'll call the livestock ranger. But your dad needs to call the police. Jump on my computer and search for the name of the farm. You'll need the exact location to give them."

"I'm on it. I'm so excited for that little girl."

"There's Dream." Michael pointed to the black horse on the screen.

"I wish it was, my little hedgehog hero, but it's just a black horse."

Katie set some sweet tea on the side table by Grandpa. "If the pony is there, maybe Dream is there somewhere too."

Selah looked up from the computer. A sickening thought caused her heart to skip a beat. Were there still horses in the barn? Dream could be in the barn. Nobody but Selah could get Sweet Dream out of a burning barn. A weakness overwhelmed her, and all the joy at finding the pony drained from her body.

Days went by before the police had access to the burned area. The barn manager had bought the pony at auction in March, and a positive identification was made using its veterinarian records. Batman's little girl was already on her way to California with a horse trailer.

When the barn manager assured the police there was only one black horse at her barn, it greatly relieved Selah. Except Batman was coming home and Sweet Dream wasn't. The manager was understanding about being grilled on seeing any black horses at the auction. Unfortunately, it was too long ago, and she had to admit she just didn't remember.

CHAPTER TWENTY-FIVE

EMMA AND BLACK VELVET

*E*mma hated that the best summer of her whole life had slipped away. Now homework crowded her riding time. Still, she was so happy with her amazing horse, she didn't even care when the major pain in her class made fun of her. His favorite thing was to move his mouth like he was talking, but no sound came out. He'd laugh and cut up with his friends. Today, she pretended to talk like him. That made everyone laugh even louder. Boys were goofs. But she had the best-best horse in the world, and she didn't care about anything else. For once, her middle name actually described what her heart was full of—Joy!

When the bus stopped at her house, she could hardly wait for the door to open. As she hurried down the steps, Velvet greeted her with a trumpeted whinny. *Joy!* "I'm coming." She ran to the pasture.

After properly greeting the most beautiful, amazing, wonderful black mare ever, Emma skipped lightheartedly to the house. She found Mom bent over the sewing machine in her office. The diffuser ran full blast infusing a lavender flower scent. "Hi, Mom." Emma's chest expanded with a deep contented breath.

"It's wonderful to see you so cheerful." Mom cut the thread on her project. "I would never have believed how good this horse has been for you. I know you like having friends with the same interests."

Emma nodded.

"You have grown so confident using your voice, and your speech is getting smoother every day."

"I talk to Velvet all the time. I don't even think about how it sounds when I talk to her. I still can't talk her into a horse trailer though."

"Has a mind of her own, does she? Like anyone we know? Come, give me a hug." Mom chuckled.

Emma melted into Mom's hug. "Being with her makes me crazy happy. I adore her."

"I never thought I would say this, but so do I."

As the weeks turned into months, Emma thought her life with Velvet made her the luckiest girl in the whole wide world. Her packages under the Christmas tree all had the theme—the year of the horse. A horse game, horse books, a T-shirt with a prancing black horse, and a new safety vest since she'd outgrown the first one. Best Christmas ever.

Even the January bluster of wind and cold didn't keep her away from Velvet. As she came in from the pasture, Mom gathered her purse and keys. "Dad said you want to go to the feed store. I need to run an errand. Want to ride along?"

"Thanks, Velvet needs a salt lick." Emma rushed to her room to get her cash stash and jumped into the car.

Mom let her out at the feed store. "I'll be back in ten. Will that give you enough time?"

"Never enough time at Kim's. Her place smells like an old barn full of molasses sweet feed."

"Ten." Mom's chuckle burst into a laugh. "It does my heart good to see you so happy."

Emma wandered the aisles. Kim's carried everything. A rack of seed packets towered next to a wooden shelf of supplies for raising chickens. The horse section had bottles and tins of remedies for every ailment from thrush to colic. Most were covered in a thin layer of dust. Halters, lead ropes, bits, girths, and saddle pads hung on the long wall. As she bent to get a salt block, the overly plump calico cat brushed against her leg. She drifted along, content in her happy place.

Next to the door hung a bulletin board always plastered with flyers. She'd made many wish lists for Santa from the horses-for-sale ads.

Her heart stopped. What she saw made the blood drain from her face. Her body tingled as if an arctic wind had blown through the store. Pinned to the board was a flyer with a picture that looked exactly like Velvet. *Can't be Velvet.* STOLEN was printed in big block letters across the top. *Stolen?* A blonde girl rode the horse without a saddle or a bridle. Her arms stretched wide like an eagle in flight. Her face reflected a happy heart. *They look amazing together.* The camera caught the horse's pink mane fluttering in the wind.

Emma trembled and couldn't catch her breath. She looked quickly around and plopped the salt block on the shelf. Plucking the thumbpins from its corner, she jerked the flyer off the board. While she clutched it in both hands, her mouth hung open while horror flooded every cell of her body. Her legs wobbled. *No mistake. It is Velvet.*

As Mom stepped into the feed store, the bell dangling on the doorknob tinkled. Emma spun to face Mom, tucking the flyer out of sight.

"You ready?"

"Ah...yes," she stammered. "I have to pay."

"I'll wait in the car."

As soon as Mom let the door close, Emma pulled the flyer out and checked again. She would know her anywhere. *It is still Velvet.* Her beautiful face and chocolate eyes. Her long forelock and thick mane. *But she belongs to me, and I have a bill of sale to prove it.* She folded the flyer and stuck it in her jeans.

When Emma set the salt lick on the counter, Kim slipped it into a paper bag. "Two thirty-five," she said loudly. "Anything wrong, Emma? You're so quiet today."

If she tried to speak, she'd choke on her words, and her voice would betray her fear. She gave a quick shake of her head. She needed to be with her horse—now.

She hurried through the store to the car. The salt block felt like a boulder in her lap. She tilted her head back, closed her eyes, and pretended to be sleepy. Mom sang praise songs along with the radio on the way home. Emma yanked out her hearing aid.

The yelling in her head—*Not your horse!*—sent Emma racing for the pasture the minute the car stopped. She threw her arms around the startled horse's neck. "That other girl sold you. You're mine, mine. No one can take you." She sobbed into Velvet's mane until there wasn't a tear left. "I'm nothing without you."

"Shoe polish." In that moment, she hated pink with all her heart. She ran for the house and dug in her dad's shoe kit till she found liquid black. She grabbed paper towels and raced to the pasture where she drenched the telltale pink in black.

In the utility room sink, she slathered blue dish soap on her hands, scrubbed, and rinsed. The black on her hands lightened, but stubbornly refused to disappear. She tried again with rough bar soap, but nothing would wash away her pain.

Dressed for bed, she sat in the dark of her room, staring into the pasture. The full moon perched low in the sky, reflecting enough light for her to watch Velvet graze. Wasn't Christmas a few weeks ago? It wasn't fair that the only thing she ever wanted was her horse, and now... Was Velvet really her horse? Or would a policeman show up one day and take them both away? Velvet to her old home and her to jail for hiding the horse. She shivered. As she pulled a blanket around her, she flopped onto her side. Closing her eyes didn't stop her mind from searching for answers. The torment in her heart urged her to find Dad. As she walked by her dresser, she snatched the pink hair ribbons for her braids, wadded them up, and cannonballed them into the trash.

The reading light was on in Dad's office so she eased the door open and peeked in.

"Come in, Emma," he signed. "I've been expecting you. You hardly ate anything at dinner. What's on your mind?"

As she curled in his lap, her head rested on his chest. She couldn't hold her tears.

Dad hugged her tight as she sobbed. When she quieted, he handed her a tissue. "What's wrong?"

She sniffed and blew. With a sigh, she unfolded the flyer and watched his face. His eyebrows arched, and he pursed his lips. He took the paper and studied the details.

"I got it off the board at Kim's," she signed reluctantly. "I didn't want to believe it, but I'm sure it's Velvet." Her hands twisted the tissue, then waved it as she signed. "How could this happen? It's so not fair."

"No, it's not fair," Dad signed.

"I bought her. I have a bill of sale. She's mine. She's been mine since March." Emma counted the months on her fingers. "Nine, no ten, months. She's mine!" Her hands flew. "When you accidentally buy a horse that's been stolen, does it belong to you or the first owner?"

Dad's expression prepared her for the bad news. "It's not so much a matter of legalities as it is doing the right thing."

She stared at the black polish under her fingernails and in the crevasses of her hands. She could try to hide Velvet with black dye, but it would never change who really owned the mare. *My horse. Only my horse. Forever my horse.*

She snatched the flyer and ran to her room.

For two days, Emma carried the flyer in her pocket. It wasn't her imagination that the atmosphere in her house was full of tension. Dad and Mom always seemed to be watching her. Were they waiting for her to do the right thing? She and Velvet couldn't hide from the truth. Emma unfolded and flattened the awful flyer on the table. Her hand poised over the phone. *I can't. I don't want to. It can't be Velvet, but I have to find out. Maybe the girl got another*

horse and doesn't even care about the one she lost anyway. Lots of black mares in the world. We can't both love the same one. Velvet's not her horse—she loves me.

She dialed the phone. When a girl answered, Emma hung up.

CHAPTER TWENTY-SIX

SELAH

*T*he New Year passed, still with no news of Sweet Dream and no hope. Selah wandered aimlessly out to the barn. Without the horse smell, it offered her no comfort, and she returned to the house. As she walked in the kitchen door, the phone rang. She waved at Mom and picked it up. Silence was the answer to her hello. "Hello," she said louder when she heard breathing. This time there was a sharp click as the caller hung up. "Strange."

Dad slipped a casserole into the oven.

"The caller ID says it's an area code from the Lufkin area. I should call back." Annoyed thoughts crowded her mind.

"Just kids with nothing better to do. Let it go."

As the family finished dinner, the phone rang. Silence again met Selah's hello. "Who is this?" she asked, frustrated.

A timid, halting voice spoke. "Can I talk to S–Selah?" The caller slurred the *S*.

"This is Selah."

"My name is Emma." Then silence. Selah frowned, wondering if the caller had hung up. "I saw a flyer for a lost horse. Have you found her?"

"She wasn't lost. Someone stole her from a horse show in Houston last February. Do you know something about her?"

"Ah… I don't think so. I feel so awful for you because she looks like my horse, and I know how I'd feel. But it can't be the same horse." Silence hung between them. "I bought her at an auction, and I live hours and hours from Houston."

"My Sweet Dream is a six-year-old mare. She's afraid of birds and horse trailers. She can open latches or jump like a deer if she wants out of the pasture. Because she's so curious, she'll investigate everything by taking a bite." Selah stopped to take a breath.

"Would you say that again slower? I couldn't understand."

"My Sweet…"

"Your horse sounds like a character," Emma said. "So is mine. She can open latches. She's super scared of birds too, but she's brave because she saved my dad when dogs attacked us."

The girl spoke carefully and seemed to struggle with enunciating the *S*s.

"Has your horse ever ripped the back pocket off your jeans?"

"She did! She wanted my peanut butter sandwich. Did yours do that too?"

"What did you say your name was?"

"Emma."

"Where do you live?"

"In Lufkin."

"Does the mare have pink-colored streaks in her mane?"

After several moments with no response, Selah asked again. "Emma? I need to know."

"Her mane was black when I bought her." A quiet pause. "Then I noticed pink showing through some black coating."

"Oh, Emma! Thank you so much for calling. I think you have my Sweet Dream. If it's her, there's a big reward for returning her. It will cover the price you paid to rescue her from the auction and all your expenses. Plus, you'll be able to buy any horse you want. I'd given up hope of ever finding her. Thank you so *soooo* much."

Emma blew a couple short, raspy breaths before she hung up. Selah's finger poised over the redial button when Dad sat down beside her. "A girl in Lufkin bought a horse at auction that sounds like Dream right down to the pink mane."

"I heard."

"She talks kinda strange, and she sounds like she's Davy's age." Selah latched onto Dad's arm. "Can you take me to Lufkin? I *have* to see the horse. I'm *sure* it's Sweet Dream."

"Can't they email—or message or something—a picture?"

"I guess. But she described the horse, and it sounded exactly like Dream. Hates trailers, scared of birds, pulls the pockets off her jeans. Has pink in her mane. It all fits. It's Dream."

"Sounds like her."

"We've got to get her." She hugged herself. "My heart knows it's Dream."

"We don't know anything for sure. Then we'd need an address. But we also don't have a truck available."

"What? Why?"

"Katie took Grandpa's truck to town to get feed. It overheated, and the check engine light came on. Garage said it needed new gaskets, and they can't get to it till next week."

"Can you take me anyway?"

"Slow down. Let's see a picture before we dash off on a wild horse hunt."

When the phone rang again, Selah glanced at the number before she grabbed it. "It's her again."

"Hello," a man said. "Is this Selah?"

"Yes, sir."

"Would it be possible for me to speak to your dad, please?"

"He's right here." She thrust the phone in his direction. Watching Dad's expressions carefully, she crushed closer. He gently held her at arm's length.

Dad frowned. "I understand. That would be difficult." He reached for a pen and paper. "Go ahead." He wrote in neat block characters. "We are about two hours out. What time would be best for you?" His eyebrows squeezed together as he nodded and listened. "I'm so sorry. This is an ordeal for both girls. See you tomorrow then."

He set the phone down with quiet care, closed his eyes, and pinched the bridge of his nose. A father's grief furrowed his brow. "Her dad thinks it's Dream. Ted's going to text me a picture in a few minutes."

"I just know it's Dream. I can't wait to get to her."

"I get it. But there's more to it." He slowly released a deep shaky breath. "He said the horse has been amazing for his daughter. Giving her confidence and companionship. She joined 4-H and, for the first time, has friends because of the horse. Emma's deaf, and she's only ten. If this is Dream, it will rip her up."

"That's hard, but it ripped me up too." *And Dream is still my horse.*

His phone buzzed. She held her breath. *It must be Dream.* He rotated the phone to show her.

"It's Dream!" Selah screeched. Her hands flew to her mouth. "It's Dream." A huge smile diverted the tears rolling down her cheeks toward her ear. She balled her fists and pumped them with explosive excitement. "Mom!" She raced through the house. "We found Dream!"

Mom tossed the load of folded towels on the couch to catch Selah in a hug. "Wonderful news. You never gave up. I'm so excited for you."

Selah ran toward her empty pasture. She threw her arms to the heavens with her fingers splayed and bowed her head. Like air seeps from a balloon, she slumped to the ground, and months of pain racked her body.

Before the sun came up, Selah popped a pod into the coffee maker. She hurried down the hall and knocked on her parents' bedroom door.

"What? It's five thirty in the morning." Dad sounded a bit grumpy.

"But you said we could leave by six."

Silence.

"I'm ready, and I'm making your coffee." She used her sweetest voice.

"I'm coming."

Then she ran back to the kitchen to wait. As Dad came in, he stretched his neck and yawned. She handed him a travel cup of coffee and a warm blueberry bagel.

He yawned deeper and would've sat in a kitchen chair except she tugged on his sleeve and offered him the car keys.

"I give up. Let's go."

Two hours later, Dad parked in front of a modest, brick two-story house, and she scanned the area for Dream. Dad went to the front door, but she walked around the side. When she spotted a girl on a horse, she stopped and stood in the cover of a shrub. A thin girl with shoulder-length, caramel-blonde hair sat bareback on the horse. She wrapped her arms around its neck and buried her face in the horse's mane. Then the girl slipped off and walked along the fence.

Dream. Selah's heart called to the horse. She closed her eyes. *Thank you, God. I'm sorry for every time I doubted. Thank you.* Tears gushed freely. The horse walked with its head low and in step with the girl. The girl offered the horse a treat, all the while rubbing the mare's neck. A pang of hurt and a twinge of betrayal mixed with mad scrambled Selah's spirit. *Did you forget about us, Dream?* She wiped her tears as she ran to the front door. Emma's dad stepped outside and shook hands with her dad.

"Hello, Ted. This is Selah." Dad drew her near.

Fighting to keep her emotions under control, all she could do was nod.

"Nice to meet you. Emma's around back. Shall we?" Ted led the way and escorted them to the pasture gate.

Selah gripped Dad's arm and whispered urgently, "It's her, Dad. It's Dream."

"You need to be absolutely sure."

"I'm sure." The delight in her voice rang clear when she called, "Dream!"

The mare threw up her head and spun to look at Selah. As Dream took a step forward, her whinny shook her whole body.

The horse trumpeted another whinny and lifted into a prance with her eyes fixed on Selah. When Emma tugged on the lead rope and rested her hand on Dream, the horse quieted. The mare attentively tipped her nose to Emma, and they walked together to the gate.

Tears running down her cheeks, Selah repeated, "My Dream." When Selah got to the gate, Emma's eyes were red and tear-filled. Awareness of Emma's pain kept Selah from flying to her horse. As she remembered her own crushing loss, Selah's heart connected with the younger girl. Selah opened the gate and went directly to Emma, wrapping her in a grateful hug.

"Thank you so much. Dream looks amazing. I can see you've taken such good care of her." Selah's gaze never left Emma's eyes. "So many awful things could have happened if you hadn't rescued her."

Dream sniffed Selah, then stuck and held her nose in her face.

"What's. She. Doing?" Emma spoke each word one at a time.

"Making sure it's me." Selah blew a deep breath out through her nose into Dream's nose. When the horse quietly whickered, Selah tried to control her tears, but a sob escaped. She wrapped herself around Dream's neck.

Emma ran to her dad, throwing her arms around his waist. When she spoke, nestled against his side, it was overly loud. "I have a bill of sale."

Ted tapped his finger to his lips as if indicating she should lower the volume.

"I can tell she knows you, but what if she wants to stay with me? We should know what *she* wants. She loves me, and I think she'll want to stay."

"She can't stay." Dumbfounded, Selah spun to Dad.

Emma pushed her way back to Dream's side, reclaiming the end of the lead rope. Planting herself between Dream and Selah, she signed emphatically. "We should let Velvet choose." When confusion wrinkled Selah's forehead, Emma changed to speaking. "I saw an old movie. A poor boy and a rich girl in a wheelchair claimed the same pony."

Selah shrugged, questioning.

"They got on opposite sides of a pen and called it." Her hand cupped possessively over Velvet's nose, and her eyes held a challenge.

"My horse likes you. That's plain. But this isn't a game." Feeling the need to never lose connection with her horse again, Selah stayed close and clutched a section of Dream's mane.

Not giving way an inch, Emma tucked her chin to her chest and scuffed her toe in the dirt.

Selah gently pulled the end of the rope, but Emma continued to cling to it. Selah increased the pressure, but it wasn't until Ted put his fingers on Emma's shoulder that she released it.

Selah hand-tapped the air in front of Dream, asking her to back up. Then she climbed the fence and sat on the top board. She clucked a couple times, low in her throat.

The mare side-passed to the fence where Selah waited. She slipped onto the mare's broad, familiar back and finger-combed her mane. Soon she asked her to walk, then trot. When she cued Dream for a halt, the mare stopped short, dropped her hindquarters low, and sucked backward in a flurry of steps.

Leaning on her dad, the younger girl stared at the pair as they pivoted in a flawless, reining spin, all without a saddle or bridle.

Urging the mare into a canter, Selah soared along the fence line. Her arms stretched, feeling like they floated on a summer breeze. Everything was perfect again, and her joy was boundless. Ten months of relief flooded her heart. She'd come so close to giving up all hope she would ever see Dream again.

But as she returned to the gate, standing in front of her was another girl who loved Dream too. Sharing would never work. They couldn't cut the horse in half. Still, she wanted to think of something to make it up to Emma. To show her how grateful she was for how she saved Dream.

"She knows you so well she can read your mind." A sad-faced Emma stood like a drenched kitten next to her dad.

"Dream and I are like one. We communicate in ways I can't even explain."

Ted wrapped one arm around Emma and drew her tight to him as he addressed Selah's dad. "Come get the horse as soon as you can. The longer it's here, the harder this will be."

"I understand, all too well, how difficult this is." Dad reached out and shook Ted's hand. "Our towing vehicle's in the shop so we'll need to get back to you."

Emma and her dad went into the house. Selah's horse stood watching her so Selah blew her a kiss. "What a relief to see you." When Dream nickered, Selah ran to her and hugged her neck. "I'm coming back for you as soon as I can. I hate to go, but I have to. You know I wouldn't leave you if there was any other way."

Barely in the car, she asked, "May I use your phone to call Jordan? She might trailer Dream home for us."

"Great idea." He handed her his cell phone. "I agree with Ted. Let's not prolong her pain. The sooner the horse is gone—the sooner Emma can start to heal."

"I feel terrible, but I don't know what to do. I think even trying to be a friend would hurt her right now."

"Very perceptive."

She zeroed in on Jordan's number. "Jordan. We found Dream! She's in Lufkin. I'm so excited I can hardly stand it. She acts like her sassy self, and she looks terrific. A little fat though. I didn't ask what they were feeding her, but she's definitely porked up. No worries, we can exercise it off."

Selah caught a quick breath when Jordan interrupted her stream of details, but it didn't stop her for long. "I can't slow down. The most important thing is—I need a favor. Can you come as soon as possible, like tomorrow, and take me to Lufkin to get Dream? Grandpa's truck is broken."

Dad parked at Chick-fil-A. "Lunch?"

Selah shook her head about lunch as she listened to Jordan. Putting her hand on her stomach, Selah curled her lips.

When Dad came back, she grinned. "Jordan can come. She said she can get to our house by nine o'clock. If everything goes right, we should have Dream in the horse trailer and headed home by noon. I'm so not going to sleep tonight. What if I wake and this was all a tease?" She pinched some french fries from Dad's pile. He reached into the bag and pulled out chicken nuggets for her. "Eat before you get so thin you blow away."

She dipped a nugget in sauce and sank her teeth into it. "These are the best nuggets ever."

She spent the rest of the ride home glowing and sharing the great news. "Caroline, we did it. We found Dream. It's really her. You're the best friend ever—I couldn't have made it without you."

"I wish I could go, but I have to help Dad at the clinic tomorrow. So exciting. This is what we hoped for."

Then Amanda. "You never gave up! And you were right—we found Dream. She's in Lufkin. Going to pick her up tomorrow.

She looks like all she's been doing is eating. Can you come soon to spend the night and celebrate with me and Caroline. Pizza and ice cream sundaes deluxe."

By nine o'clock the next morning, Selah waited on the porch watching for Jordan, her mind racing with anticipation and her spirit riding on joy. Jordan's truck dodged the ruts in the driveway. She backed expertly to the trailer. Selah ran to drop the tailgate. Within five minutes, they had the gooseneck hitched and were off.

As soon as Selah slipped into the cab, she spewed excitement. "Can you believe it? After all this time, she turns up in Lufkin! I'm so happy."

Jordan tried to talk. "This girl saw the flyer and..."

"In her feed store. My friend, Amanda, has an older brother. He came all the way from where I used to live and drove her and Caroline across Texas putting up flyers. And one of them worked! I'd really given up."

"Have you had coffee?" Jordan pulled onto the highway.

"Of course not. That stuff is nasty."

"You mean I'm going to listen to this jet stream of excitement for the next two hours?"

"Could be." Selah grinned. "I won't have time to get Dream in shape to do the demonstrations at the show next weekend, but by April, we'll be ready to rock. I'm getting a padlock for her stall, and I'm never letting her out of my sight again. I'll get a cot and sleep in front of the stall."

"I'm happy for you. You and Sweet Dream have such a special bond. Losing your best friend is the worst. How's the other girl taking it?"

The blur of grass on the side of the road blotted out everything except what she knew Emma must be feeling. "Not good."

CHAPTER TWENTY-SEVEN

SELAH AND SWEET DREAM

When they arrived at Emma's house, Selah pulled her stocking hat over her ears and headed to the front door. Jordan waited in the truck. Emma's dad came out before she knocked and directed her to the back. "Emma has said her goodbyes and doesn't think she can watch the horse leave. I figure you can handle this on your own."

"Yes, sir. Thank you. I'm so very sorry about this. And grateful for everything Emma's done." Anxious to see Dream, Selah hurried to the pasture. She leaned against the mare, needing to feel her close. "I've missed you with every beat of my heart." She stretched one arm around Dream's chest and draped the other over her back. As her face rested on the mare's withers, the horse wrapped her neck around her resting her muzzle near her waist. Dream smelled earthy, and Selah clung to her—moving with her shallow breaths.

"Let's go home." New joy lifted her spirit when the mare extended her head and tipped her nose for Selah to slip on the halter. As she led Dream away, the mare looked back at the house. "Aww, you like Emma, don't you?"

Demonstrating years of relationship and her trust in Selah, Dream stepped up beside her in the horse trailer without a moment's hesitation. Selah patted the mare and secured her inside.

Jumping back into the truck, Jordan put it in gear and started off.

Selah spotted Emma in the side mirror. "Stop."

Emma stood in the driveway behind them shivering like a baby bird with broken wings. The utter defeat on her face pained Selah. She opened the door and hurried to the younger girl who looked so lost. As Selah gushed appreciation, she closed her eyes and hugged Emma tight. "I know this is hard and terrible. I'm so sorry. Thank you for rescuing her. I'm grateful—*forever*."

"Why don't you introduce us, Selah?" Jordan asked.

Selah stepped back. "Emma, this is Jordan. She's my instructor."

"I'm glad to meet you," Jordan said as Ted joined them. "I know Selah explained there is a sizeable reward for Sweet Dream's return. Have you heard of my boss, Mr. Cooper?"

Emma shook her head.

"He's an amazing trainer, and he trained Dream. She was with us at a show when she was stolen. With the reward he's putting up, you can buy a great horse. Plus, have enough to never need to worry about the cost of keeping a horse. The offer is that generous."

The girl dragged her fingers from her lips toward Jordan, signing the expected thank you.

"I have an idea." Selah brightened and jiggled Jordan's arm. "Mr. Cooper offered to give me Gringo. Maybe he'd loan him to Emma instead?"

"Selah, you should talk to Mr. Cooper before you give Gringo away."

"He couldn't have a better home, but you're right." Selah slid her hand onto the younger girl's shoulder. "Not to worry, I'll think of a way to work it out with Mr. Cooper. You'd love Gringo. He's a buckskin, and he's beautiful and sweet and trained just like Dream. It would give you time to horse shop and find the perfect horse for you."

Emma stared at the bold pink lettering on the trailer—Sweet Dream. She looked down, but not before the tears gleamed in her eyes. Emma's dad put his arm around her, and she leaned on him as they turned away.

Selah nearly gagged on her happy, feeling like an awful person when it was the worst day of Emma's life. As Selah got back into the truck, her heart ached. "I know just how she feels, and it hurts—bad. The shock—the pain—hopeless and helpless." She bit her lip, remembering her darkest days and knowing Emma was going through the same thing—except without hope. Dream would never return to her.

Arriving home with her lost horse felt like the year Mom made pumpkin pie but left out the sugar. It looked beautiful, your mouth watered as you put whipped cream on top, but the delight was missing. Selah couldn't bring herself to enjoy her own happy when she knew firsthand how much Emma hurt.

When Dream backed from the trailer, her head stretched high, and her muscles tensed.

As Jordan closed the trailer doors, she advised Selah, "I'd ask the vet to check her out and recommend a diet. She's had way too much grass for too long."

"I'm sure Grandpa will come look at her soon. Bye, Jordan. Thank you a million times."

Looking around, Sweet Dream pricked her ears forward as she belted out a whinny.

"Calling Buddy? I'll get him for you soon." Starting for the pasture gate, the mare broke into an excited trot, dragging Selah along on the lead rope. She didn't have the heart to correct the mare's behavior. "You're happy to be home, aren't you? We'll work on your manners later."

She released the horse into the pasture. The mare whinnied and moved in a floating trot. As she circled, her tail flipped over her back. Selah leaned on the fence and admired the prancing black beauty. "Welcome home, beautiful." *We gotta work on that haybelly.* Then she thought again of Emma and her empty pasture. She had to fix that—first.

She hung up from Mr. Cooper and didn't even draw a breath before dialing Emma. "This is Selah," she said to the woman who answered. "May I talk to Emma?"

"It was nice of you to call, but I don't think that's a good idea. Emma is hurting, and I don't think it would help her to hear how the horse is doing."

"I have great news for her."

"Can you share it with me first?"

"Mr. Cooper, my trainer, has offered to give Emma lessons on Gringo. That's the horse he trained me on. My time on his ranch changed my whole life."

"This the man who offered the reward for the return of the horse?"

"Yes, ma'am."

"Sounds too good to be true."

"He feels partially responsible since Dream was in his stabling area at the show. He's been very generous and supportive. When I told him about her and what she did for Dream, he wanted to do something extra for her."

"Hang on. I'll get her."

When Emma came to the phone, Selah chattered nonstop. Emma had to keep asking her to repeat and slow down.

Maybe getting lessons on Gringo would bolster Emma's sagging spirit. "Ask your parents to call Jordan and set up the best time. You could do weekends or stay a week during a school break." Selah didn't say one word about how Dream was doing, and Emma didn't ask.

"My friends, Caroline and Amanda, worked hard to find all the stolen horses. They put up the flyer you found in the feed store. We've been talking, and we want to help other people who've had a horse stolen. It was pure luck I spotted the pony that was taken at the same time as Dream, in the news clips about a forest fire. Anyway, we thought you'd like to help."

"I'm not allowed on the internet."

"You could contact the leaders of the 4-H equestrian groups and send them flyers to distribute to their members."

"And Pony Club. We have a big club in our district."

Selah added, "You could put up flyers in the Lufkin feed stores so we don't have to drive all that way next time. I gotta go. I have to help Grandma Katie with her chores. Call Jordan. And don't be scared of Mr. Cooper. He's grouchy, but he has a puppy heart."

Selah's hand lingered on the phone. She'd done everything she could for Emma. Why did it still feel like it wasn't enough?

Despite the January wet and cold keeping her from riding Dream, Selah spent every minute possible in the barn. If not for the weather, she would have slept in the barn. It was like her tank was empty or as if the air had been sucked out of her life, and it would take more than a week to feel whole again.

The mare's heavy winter coat made her look like a wooly mammoth. "I think this is the thickest your coat's ever been. Did you think we were going to have the worst winter ever?"

As she moved the curry in circles, Grandpa stepped into the barn and pulled the big door shut behind him to block the wind. "I'm here. What did you want to show me?"

"Would you check out Dream, please? I'm worried. She's not herself. She's cranky all the time. Do you think she misses Emma?"

Grandpa shrugged.

"Her coat's super thick. She was a bit fat when I got her back so I've been trying to exercise her more, but it doesn't help. She wolfs down her food and slams her foot on the rail demanding more. I put a rock in her bucket to slow her down, but she acts like she's starving. Silly girl picks the rock out of the feed bucket with her teeth and drops it in her water bucket." Selah threw up her hands in frustration. "When I put hay in the pasture, she won't let Buddy have any unless I put the piles miles apart."

Grandpa walked around the mare and looked at her with more interest.

"Is she insulin resistant? Or have a thyroid problem? Could she have Cushing's?"

A twinkle came into his eyes, and he hid a grin with his hand.

"What's so funny?"

"Sunshine, don't get your medical advice from the internet. But I do think you should call Dr. Steve and get a professional opinion."

Two days later, Dr. Steve arrived with Caroline to examine Sweet Dream. Caroline hooked elbows with Selah, and they hovered around the vet.

"I'm so glad you came with your dad. I'm crazy worried about Dream."

"Dad's the best. He'll figure out what's going on with her. It'd be so much easier if horses would speak English."

"What if she has a broken heart? What if she wants to be with Emma?"

After several tense minutes, the vet flipped his stethoscope over his head to lay the instrument across his shoulders. As a grin appeared on his face, he turned aside.

"What? What is wrong with Dream?" Selah shrieked in confusion.

"Not one thing is wrong with her, but you should prepare a foaling stall."

"No way. She's never been bred." Dr. Steve had to be wrong.

He chuckled. "Yes, she has. She's definitely in foal. Without doing an ultrasound, I'm guessing she's due late February or early March." Dr. Steve scribbled on his clipboard. "I'll email your grandpa my recommended feeding and vitamin protocol."

Caroline squealed, grabbing Selah by the arms. "A foal! How exciting."

While Caroline bounced and celebrated, Selah kept repeating, "Can't be."

"Come on, Caroline," Dr. Steve called as he headed to the truck. "I've got two more farm calls."

"I'm so happy for you. I'll call you later."

As she watched her friend leave, Selah puzzled through the time frame, counting out on her fingers the months Dream had been missing. "Ten months—and the foal due February or March." In stunned disbelief, she marched to the house to call Emma. When the girl came to the phone, Selah struggled to be calm. "Emma? Has Dream been in the pasture with any boy horses?"

"Only once. The first night she was here. She opened her gate and jumped into Mrs. Holmes's pasture with her herd. She raises Welsh Mountain Ponies. One of them is a boy."

"A stallion?" Selah closed her eyes and gritted her teeth. *Please, not a pony stallion.*

"He's beautiful. Why do you want to know?"

She planted her elbow on the table, and her head dropped into the palm of her hand. She squeezed her temples. Suddenly, the light hurt her eyes. "Oh great." She groaned. "Just great." *So much for the spring show circuit.*

"What did you say? I couldn't hear you."

"Nothing," she mumbled and diverted the conversation. "How are your lessons going? Are you loving Gringo?"

"Love my lessons, but Mr. Cooper thinks Gringo is too much horse for me. He said I should keep coming to ride, and he would think about putting me up on Gringo again in a few months. He says I need to get a little bigger and a lot stronger."

"That's crazy. Dream's too much horse for most people, and you did great with her. Gringo's a pussycat."

"Not for me. He puts his head down to his knees and nearly pulls me out of the saddle. My one-rein-stop is too lame to keep him from doing it. Jordan has me on a sweet old mare named Kitty."

"I know Kitty. They brought her out of retirement, I guess." Selah grimaced when she remembered the damage Sweet Dream had inflicted on the gray mare as the two of them sorted out who was barn boss.

After hanging up, she trudged back to the barn through the drizzle. "What am I going to do with a pony?" Hands on her hips, she glared at Sweet Dream. "A pony? Really? What a mess you've gotten us into. Being a momma is a big responsibility, you know?" She rolled her head back and stared into the barn rafters. "Foaling stall."

She considered her options while wishing answers would fall from the sky. Dangling from a thread, a spider swayed with the air currents as it inched lower. Dream nickered to her. "Trying to get on my good side, are you? You know I can't stay mad at you." Selah laid her hand gently on the mare's belly, wondering if she could feel the foal move. "We're going to have a baby? Soon. I can't believe it," she whispered as she slid her hand to another area. Then her mouth opened in a tiny gasp of wonder. "I can feel it!" *Awesome.* "A new life and I feel her move."

Never mind the spring shows. She didn't care anymore that the foal would be part pony. "I could teach it to pull a buggy. I could train it for Davy and Michael to ride. It will be a filly! I just know it. Of course, she'll look like you." She closed her eyes and gave the mare a full-body hug. "Imagine a foal. Not just any foal, but *your* foal. I'm already in love." She ran from the barn to share the news with the whole world. One after the other, she called Caroline, Amanda, and Jordan. "I felt the foal kick!"

When Mom came home with Davy and Michael, Selah gushed, "You have to come to the barn with me. It's the most amazing thing ever." Everyone followed her to the barn, but none of them could keep up with her excitement.

She slipped a halter on Dream's head and tied her in the aisle. "Come here." She beckoned to the boys. When they looked leery, she assured them. "It's okay. She's tied, and I'm right here with you." She ran her hand down the boys' arms and grasped their wrists, placing one of their palms on the mare's belly. Sweet Dream pulled hay from a rack. Selah watched their faces for the amazement that would come soon. She was quickly rewarded when Michael's eyes lit up and Davy's mouth gaped.

"A baby horse." Michael squatted down to look under Dream. "I can see her belly move."

"A foal." Selah eased the boys back from Dream. "A special surprise gift."

CHAPTER TWENTY-EIGHT

SELAH AND SWEET DREAM

Selah stumbled half awake into the kitchen. "Morning, Dad."

"I like this new you—up in the morning. Doing chores."

"Dr. Steve said the foal could be born any day now." She tugged on her stocking cap, a sweater, a coat, and her muck boots. "Wasn't it 68 degrees yesterday?"

"I love Texas, but the weather changes by the hour. The nastiest weather we get all year is when the Houston Trail Riders gather at the rodeo." Dad sipped his coffee, lingering at the breakfast table.

"I'm debating whether I should put Dream out in the pasture in this mess or leave her and Buddy in the barn. If I leave her in, I'll need to muck the stalls before I can go, so could you give me a ride to school?"

"I can drop you on my way to work."

Selah shuddered as she stepped into the cold. Cupping her collar over her cheeks, she dashed to the barn. Buddy nickered. Dream rattled her feed bucket. Selah hurried to dump feed in their buckets.

"What—not even a nicker? Miss Extra-Grumpy today or what?" Her babbling stopped, and wonder filled her heart when she saw the wet foal lying in the bedding. "You had your baby! It looks just like you," she cooed. "I'm sad 'cause I wanted to be here. What a special moment, and I missed it. You coulda waited for me."

Dream dropped her head to the baby and licked its body vigorously. Then she nudged it. The baby balanced on its nose as it tried and failed to get up. The foal sat on its haunches with its legs splayed. Pushing up onto its hind legs, it promptly fell onto its shoulder and collapsed.

"How cute are you?"

In one more huge effort, the foal heaved itself onto its tiny hooves, popping up like an umbrella. It swayed and balanced on stiffened legs looking like a four-legged spider. When it took its first awkward step, it tumbled and rolled under Dream. Selah gasped, but Dream merely shuffled her hooves and ignored the floundering baby. This time, when it tried to stand, its rump pushed against Dream's front legs to help steady it. The foal balanced and turned its delicate head to reach its dam's udder. All was well in a perfect world.

"Are you a filly?" Selah peeked. "Yup. A real Mini-Me. A tiny beauty."

After the foal finished gorging on milk, she staggered and dropped to the floor. Selah opened the stall door and slipped inside. Dream eyed her.

"Is it okay if I touch her?" Selah moved closer to Dream and rubbed the mare. "You'll be an amazing mama." When Dream showed no sign of aggressiveness, Selah reached out tentatively to touch the foal. "What is softer than a lamb? You." She admired and stroked every inch of the foal. "We're going to be great friends." As the filly sank to her belly in the shavings, Selah knelt down with her.

"Need to go now." Dad stepped into the barn. "What's taking so long? You're already late for school. Where are you?"

"Here. On the floor in Dream's stall. Come look."

Dad smiled when he saw her cradling the foal's head in her lap. "Wow. What have you got there?" He jumped away when Dream thrust forward at him, flashing her teeth.

"Isn't she amazing?"

He nodded. "Amazing all right. Protective too."

"I mean the foal. Dream's being a good new mommy. Would you call Dr. Steve? I just can't leave her. He needs to check them both out and take care of this thing hanging from her belly."

Dad laughed. "Her umbilical cord? That's how she got nourishment from her mother until she was born." He turned to go, then paused. "I suppose you want a maternity day off from school too?"

Still stroking the foal, she flashed him a well-duh look.

She studied the foal. She traced her finger along its muzzle, around its eyes, and followed the edges of her ears. The foal's ears twitched, but she didn't wake. "What a miracle. Did you know you were knitted together in your mother's womb? You're the most precious thing ever."

When Dream dropped a pile of manure a foot from her, Selah curled her nose. With her legs cramping, she slid out from under the foal's head and stretched. As she waited for Dr. Steve, she got a bucket to hold the sac that had enveloped the foal for eleven months. Caroline had said her dad would need to inspect it to make sure all of it had been expelled at the foal's birth. Then Selah removed the muck from the stall. She was taking no chances the baby could pick up an infection.

Mom came to the barn, bearing a breakfast taco.

"Can I use your phone?"

"May I meet the baby before you rob me?" Mom teased, holding out a hand wipe and the food. "Eat first."

As Selah devoured the taco, Mom peeked at the foal.

"Watch Dream," Selah warned, stepping between them. "She's protecting the foal. Her ears are flat back."

Mom took a step away from the stall and handed Selah the phone. "Let me guess, pictures for her baby album."

She crumpled the taco wrapper and took the phone. "Thanks and thanks. Yes, and I want video of her baby steps. So adorable."

"Grandpa and Katie will come to meet the foal about the time the boys get home from school. They're so excited."

"Will you explain to the boys they have to be super quiet or Dream will freak out? She may not let anybody but me near the foal—except Grandpa. She'll let him. People think horses are dumb, but they're so wrong. Dream knows Grandpa helped save her life when she was trapped in the wire."

"I'm sure Dream is especially brilliant. Have you picked out a name?"

Selah pulled a paper from her pocket and scanned her short list. "Since I'm thinking about training her for the boys, I thought about letting them name her, but I'm afraid of what they might come up with."

"They might come up with something cute."

"They might. But it would probably be something like Hedgehog." As if on cue, the foal spurted a noise sounding like a tiny horse fart.

"Maybe Hedgehog would work after all." She giggled. "But what do you think of Arabella? It means lovely, elegant, and beautiful."

"Great name. She's all of those things. Not really a name the boys can relate to, though."

"True. That's important, but the name has to fit the filly. The boys could call her Belle if they want. I have to talk to Sweet Dream before I decide."

"You do that. Are you going to share the news with Emma?"

Selah shook her head. "She didn't know Dream was in foal. Her mom asked me not to call anymore. She says it's not helpful for Emma. Makes sense. It's too soon. I wouldn't like it if it were the other way around and Emma kept calling *me* to share good news about Dream."

CHAPTER TWENTY-NINE

SELAH AND SWEET DREAM

The more time passed, the more the name Arabella suited the precious but feisty foal.

Nearly every day, Selah spent fifteen minutes handling the filly. She wanted her to learn to be both respectful and trusting. As Selah approached Sweet Dream in the pasture, the mare raised her head with blades of grass dangling from her mouth. The four-month-old foal slept sprawled in the grass close by.

"All you do is eat. Being a mama a full-time job?" She patted the mare's neck, and Dream went back to grazing. Selah sat cross-legged in the field and watched Arabella sleep. Napping was her superpower. The foal stirred, stretched, and rolled to her belly. After lunging to her feet, the filly wobbled to Dream and nursed. "You're such a sweet mama. I'm so proud of you. If you hadn't come home when you did, I would have missed this amazing time with you."

Selah's delight lifted the corners of her mouth in a wide smile. When she inhaled, she felt as if she was breathing joy instead of air. After the foal's belly filled with milk, Selah eased to her and scratched her withers. Cupping her love for the foal in her hands, she worked her way all over its body. "I completely adore you."

As she scratched the base of the foal's tail, Arabella wiggled her little rump. "Oh, that's your sweet spot."

The foal scooted backward when Selah pretended to be done scratching.

"What would you say if I trained you to become a therapy horse? All you need is charm, but you're super smart too. You're easy to handle, and you love to play. I could teach you some fun tricks, and we could go to the children's hospital to cheer them up. Rump scratching could be one of your best tricks. Davy and Michael won't mind sharing you with other kids."

Then, with a playful hop-jump, the filly bounded to her dam's side. Dream's filly suckled like a greedy hummingbird while Selah rambled on about her pony career plans.

"And we could have Read to a Pony Day at the library. You're already great at it. Your sleeping snort is like punctuation." Her favorite pastime had become reading to Arabella. With her back against a round bale of hay and one hand on the sleeping filly, Selah read to her from a collection of horse stories.

When the young horse would wake, she followed her around the pasture snapping one picture after another—each one more darling than the last. "Funny. When I first learned you were about to arrive, I was upset. Because of you, Dream and I will miss the Spring Exposition. But now, I can't imagine life without your cuteness. You're the second best thing to ever happen to me." She kissed the filly's muzzle. "I'm so grateful for you. You could be a Breyer Horse Model. I'm going to pick your cutest pictures and send them to the selection committee. I wonder if Miss Cindy would like some pictures too. She might want to make a movie about you. Ah...the plans I have for you. It will be a wonderful life."

As Arabella turned five months old, Selah had a serious talk with Dream. "Arabella's a big girl now. Time to wean her. What if I move you to Grandpa's and leave her here with Buddy? He'll watch out for her and so will I." As she chatted with Dream, the filly flipped her tail and streaked in energetic circles in the pasture. Dashing to Buddy, she snatched a bite of hay right from under his nose. "Buddy's just like Grandpa. He spoils Arabella like Grandpa spoils me. Everybody should have a grandpa like mine."

Selah rubbed tiny circles on Dream's shoulder. "Dream. There's something else I've been thinking about. Something important. This will hurt. Maybe the hardest thing—*ever*. Maybe we can't do it. But I feel like we should talk about it."

With one arm over Dream's back and the other cupped across her chest, Selah drew strength to explain what was on her heart. "I've been making big plans for Arabella. I want to teach her to pull a cart, be a safe ride for Davy and Michael. Teach her everything she needs to know to be the best therapy horse. But it was right under my eyes all along, and I missed it."

Dream took a step away and dropped her head to graze. One hand still resting on the mare, Selah moved with her, keeping the connection she needed between them. "Or I didn't see it because

I don't want to let her go. But I have you. Thanks to Emma. She has nobody. Emma and Gringo just couldn't work it out. You know how it is. There's one special horse for every person and one special person for every horse." Her voice cracked.

"Did I tell you Arabella also means answered prayer? What if she's Emma's answered prayer? I've been thinking." She swallowed hard and sniffed.

"After she's weaned and all—not right away, but after—we should give Arabella to Emma." Selah bit down on her bottom lip, determined to be strong. "What do you think, Dream? You know Emma would love Arabella as much as she loved you."

After her long talk, Selah felt like Dream agreed with the plan. She knew what she had to do. Even so, her eyes brimmed as the phone rang. *I could hang up. Emma would never know. But I would. It's the right thing. What good is love if you don't share it?*

When Emma's mom answered, Selah swallowed and squeaked out a hello.

"Hello, Selah. How can I help you?"

"I wanted to tell you Dream had a filly. We're weaning her now."

"That's nice."

She sounds a bit abrupt.

"We all hope it goes well with you and Dream and her new filly."

"I've named her Arabella. She looks just like Dream, except the vet says she'll be closer to the sire's size than to Dream's."

"I'm happy for you. Did Emma know the horse was pregnant?"

"Not unless she connected the dots when I asked her if Dream had been with any boy horses."

"Not likely. I think it would be best if I don't share the news with her then. Thank you for setting up the riding lessons for

Emma. She loves going, and you were right about how much she'd learn at—"

Selah interrupted, "Dream and I want to give Arabella to Emma." Unsure how to interpret the sudden silence on the phone, she pulled it away from her ear, looked at it, and put it back. *Did she hang up? Hate the idea?*

Then came a soft sniffle. Soon Emma's mom was ugly crying. "Call—you later." She choked back tears and hung up.

Several hours later, Emma called. "Velvet had a baby!"

"And she's beautiful. She looks just like her momma." Selah made sure to enunciate every word for Emma.

"Can you send me a picture?"

"I want you to come meet her instead."

Emma was quiet.

"Emma?"

"I think it would hurt too much. Could I just get a picture of Velvet, I mean S—weet Dream, with the foal?"

"Her name is Arabella."

"That's beautiful."

"Please come, Emma. You have to come."

CHAPTER THIRTY

SELAH AND SWEET DREAM

Three days later, Selah brushed and combed Arabella while they waited for Emma to arrive. The more she thought about the two of them together, the more Selah knew they would make a perfect pair. The filly was beautiful and smart like Dream, but she was much more trusting and agreeable. Arabella was more of a sweetheart than a troublemaker. Anxious to see them interact and wanting the filly to make a good first impression, Selah brushed her all over for the second time. Once she saw them—well, then she'd know for sure.

"Someone special is coming to meet you. She will love you with all her heart. If you love her too, then you'll have a girl of your own. She'll take special care of you—forever. Wouldn't you like that?" She slipped around the filly, picking up each tiny hoof. "But if you don't like her, you tell me. We won't let you go if it makes you unhappy."

Grandpa appeared at her side. "Thought you might need a little moral support."

She nodded but refused to cry. "I do."

"You've done a wonderful job with this filly. Not many horses get the great start in life that you've given her."

"Everything you taught me. Wait here. I have something for you." She scooted to the barn and returned with a bright green gift bag.

"What's this?"

"Open it."

Grandpa rustled the tissue paper aside and pretended he might be sticking his hand in a viper's den. Finally, he pulled out an unusual, green tweed cap. "What is this?"

"It's handmade from Irish wool. For your trip to Ireland, so you'll look like you belong there instead of like a cowboy."

"I can't wear my Stetson?"

Smiling, she shook her head. "Have so much fun, Grandpa."

When Caroline arrived, she hurried straight to Selah and held her in a tight hug. "The big day."

"Thanks for coming. I want to make it a celebration. Like when someone gets married."

"When Emma gets here, I'm gonna FaceTime with Amanda. She did so much to help find Dream. She needs to share this with us. I wish she'd move here too."

The girls quieted as a car drove slowly down the gravel road and parked by the barn. Selah swallowed the lump in her throat but wished she'd never made the call. She loved Arabella. *How can I give her away?*

Grandma Katie arrived right behind Emma's family and took Grandpa's arm. He tipped his new Irish cap to Selah. After Selah's parents and brothers joined the group, Emma's dad introduced her mom and sister and their neighbor Mrs. Holmes. When Caroline held up the phone screen, Selah waved at a grinning Amanda. "Thank you," she mouthed to her friends.

As soon as Selah saw Emma's solemn face, she wondered if she'd done the right thing insisting Emma come. But the instant Emma glimpsed Arabella, her gloom vanished. Then Dream whickered.

"She remembers me!" Emma exclaimed, clapping with joy.

"Of course, she does." In American Sign Language, Selah signed, "She's happy to see you." She'd studied to talk better with Emma.

Emma walked to Dream and rubbed her forehead. As she stepped closer to the mare, Dream wrapped her neck around Emma and pressed her in a horse hug. Soon she nuzzled Emma's pockets.

"Yes. I have carrot cookies." Emma flattened her hand and offered a treat.

When Arabella squealed, Emma turned to her. "Who are you? You want a cookie too?" Extending her nose to Emma, Arabella was rewarded with a cookie. "You're too adorable," Emma was breathless. The filly turned her head to follow Emma's every move. Emma cooed and whispered to her.

Pleased with their interaction, Selah asked, "What do you think? Is she the cutest ever?"

Seemingly lost in her own wonderful world, Emma didn't answer. Her hands rested lightly on the filly, and her soft blissful expression delighted Selah.

Selah touched Emma's arm. When she had her full attention, she asked again, "Isn't she the cutest ever?"

Emma crossed her fists over her chest, and Selah understood that meant love. Besides, the look on Emma's face said it all.

Emma and Arabella belonged together. Selah flipped over her hand and motioned toward Emma. "Sweet Dream and I want you to have Arabella."

When Emma didn't react or respond, her dad signed what Selah had signed and said. Emma looked frozen. Then, as if someone pulled strings tied to her body, she lifted and came to life. Her hands flew in conversation with her parents, her voice adding guttural sounds.

Grandma Katie sniffled. Next to her, Mrs. Holmes blinked hard and blew her nose.

Selah's mom stood beside her, offering the strength of her support for the most difficult and grown-up thing Selah had ever been challenged to do. "I'm so proud of you. What an amazing selfless act of love."

Emma moved her head and a balled fist in unison telling Selah yes.

Mrs. Holmes spoke to Emma. "How exciting. She could stay in my pasture with my weanlings so she wouldn't be alone."

"Perfect." Selah stayed focused on what was best for Arabella. "We wouldn't want her to grow up to be a super-brat. They learn important things, like manners, from each other in the first couple years. And Jordan promised to train the filly to ride when she's old enough."

"Maybe you and I could do it together," Emma spoke carefully and clearly. "And since we both love the same horses, we'll be horse friends forever."

Selah wrapped Emma in a hug. "Forever."

The End

Dear Reader:

If you enjoyed this book, please take a minute to help other people find it by sharing a review.

Sign up on my website for new release notification so you will find out about the next book as soon as it is available. Also, for any contests or giveaways— join me at http://www.susancount.com/

Hearing from readers encourages me to keep writing. E-mail a comment: susancountauthor@yahoo.com

Please like Susan Count at http://www.facebook.com/ susancount where I post only horse related horse-related videos.

I'm also on Pinterest: https://www.pinterest.com/susancount/

Award Winning
DREAM HORSE ADVENTURES
Series

MARY'S SONG-BOOK 1
A girl and a foal share one thing. They are both
lame. One cannot survive without the other.

SELAH'S SWEET DREAM-BOOK 2
A girl with a dream to be an equestrian
superstar. A horse with ATTITUDE.

SELAH'S PAINTED DREAM-BOOK 3
One word can ruin a perfect life—moving.

SELAH'S STOLEN DREAM-BOOK 4
One girl's victory is the other's tragic defeat.

READER REVIEWS:
Best horse books ever. Charming. Action packed.
Heart-warming. Page turner. I'm utterly smitten.
Stole my heart. Good for the soul.

ABOUT WRITING...

How many twists and turns can one person take before they figure out what they were born to do? Nothing prepared me to write novels for children. But the writing process gave me great joy and restored my spirit after a season of loss.

The passion behind my work is renewed from letters that come from young fans. One recently told me she felt like she was riding in the buggy with Mary and Laura in *Mary's Song*. A grandmother admonished me to stop saying the books are juvenile fiction because she adored them and it made her feel like she was twelve-years-old again. Love from fans keeps me writing.

I adore grandchildren, horses, bunnies, mochas, the beach, forest trails, and especially joy found in the Lord. Instilled with the need to create, I love writing adventure stories. I am a lifelong equestrian and am owned by a Rocky Mountain Horse. Though I am a rider and lover of horses, I make no claims of expertise in any riding discipline, and each book requires thorough research to avoid annoying those who would know.

I write at an antique secretary desk that occupies a glass room with a forest view. Fittingly, it once belonged to the same wise grandmother who introduced me to the love of reading via Walter

Farley's horse books. That desk has *secret* compartments, which hold memories, mysteries, and story ideas.

The only thing more fun than riding might be writing horse adventure stories, and I invite you to saddle up and ride along.

CONTENTS

Made in the USA
Monee, IL
31 March 2022